ROLE PERFORMANCE OF ADULT EDUCATION TEACHERS
PROBLEMS AND PROSPECTS

ROLE PERFORMANCE OF ADULT EDUCATION TEACHERS

PROBLEMS AND PROSPECTS

DR. G. LOKANADHA REDDY
Senior Lecturer, Adult and Non-formal Education,
Department of Education,
Alagappa University,
Tamil Nadu

DISCOVERY PUBLISHING HOUSE
NEW DELHI—110 002

Published by:

DISCOVERY PUBLISHING HOUSE PVT. LTD.
4383/4B, Ansari Road, Darya Ganj
New Delhi-110 002 (India)
Phone : +91-11-23279245; 23253475; 43596065
E-mail : discoverybooksindia@gmail.com
discoverypublishinghouse@gmail.com
web : www.discoverypublishinggroup.com

***First Published:* 2003**

***Reprinted:* 2021**

ISBN: 978-81-7141-390-4

Role Performance of Adult Education Teachers
Problems and Prospects

Printed at:
Infinity Imaging Systems
Delhi

Contents

Foreword

The book in your hands entitled "Role Performance of Adult Education Teachers : Problems and Prospects" is written by Dr. G. Lokanadha Reddy of S.V. University, Tirupati, A.P. State. There are a few books dealing with the education of adults. But books focussing on Adult education teachers and their role performance are very megre.

The adult education teachers are expected to perform various roles such as — organiser of the center, teacher of literacy, dissemination of functional information, mobiliser of resources, professional devotion, guidance and counselling. To perform the above said multidimensional roles effectively, they have to carryout several activities under different marked situations. In carrying out these activities, the teachers may come across varied problems in different marked situations. The present book provides valuable information on the different roles and activities of the adult education teachers, the variety of the problems they are facing in different specific situations and the practical solutions in overcoming the same. Based on the above, the relevant strategies in designing curriculum for pre-service and in service training of adult education teachers are also highlighted in the book.

Hence the present book is highly useful source material and helpful guide to the programme planners, implementers, administrators, researchers and students who are involved in strengthening the literacy programmes for different groups in the society.

Prof. S. Padmanabaiah
Head and Dean
Faculty of Education
S.V. University, Tirupati
Andhra Pradesh

Acknowledgements

I express my sincere gratitude to Dr. M.V. Sudhakara Reddy, Reader, Department of Adult Education, for his guidance and encouragement towards the period of present investigation.

I am thankful to Dr. V.L.N. Reddy, Professor, Department of Adult Education, for providing necessary facilities in the department to carryout the present investigation.

I wish to record my sincere thanks to the Project Officers of Sri Kalahasti and Naidupet Projects for giving me permission to carry the research work in various centres of the Projects.

I am extremely grateful to Supervisors and Instructors of the above Projects for their co-operation in the collection of data. I am thankful to Mr. P. Balasiddamuni, Lecturer in Statistics, S.V. University College, for his advise on statistical techniques.

Lastly but not in the least, I wish to express my thanks to staff members and research scholars of the Dept. of Adult Education who extended their co-operation and help for the comletion of the present study.

G. Lokanadha Reddy

1

Introduction

The teacher or instructor is pivot of the educational system. The whole process of education revolves round the teacher or instructor.

The teacher or instructor is expected to play many roles whether he is working in formal system or non-formal system. He has instructional responsibilities, counselling responsibilities, professional growth responsibilities,.curriculum development responsibilities, public relations responsibilities and others as well. Teaching places a multiplicity demands on teacher or instructor talents. The various roles that the teacher must play are not even always compatible with one another. Consequently many teachers feel a good deal of pressure as they attempt to deal with day-to-day requirements of their profession. Today, the successful teacher must be able to shoulder many responsibilities, adapt to many situations, and exercise leadership under a multitude of circumstances. The profession requires individuals who are strong-willed yet adaptable to a wide variety of conditions.

Actually in recent years, the instructional role of the teacher has changed from a dispenser of information to that of an instructional manager. As an instructional manager, the teacher is responsible for creating an environment where learning can take place. In this role teachers determine learning objectives, diagnose learners, plan learning activities, implement programmes, and evaluate learners progress.

The roles of the teacher or the instructor in formal or non-formal education may be the same, that of instruction responsibilities, counselling responsibilities, professional growth responsibilities, curriculum development responsibilities, and public relations responsibilities. But, in approach the instructor of adults must be a diversified person because of dealing with the beings already having some life experiences. He must develop friendly approach to the adult learners. The main aim of the programme is to provide functional information along with literacy. So, the adult education instructor should acquire some basic knowledge about various occupational groups to promote the professional skills of the adult learners.

Further, in adult education guidance is one of the important function of the instructor. The adult learner, as a laymen seeks guidance on various areas like personal and social problems, study habits learning problems, information regarding the developmental programmes etc.

Thus, the adult education instructor is different from that of the formal school teacher. Of course both are meant for the development of human beings. But, formal school teacher activities are mainly concerned to the school and activities of adult education instructor are extended to the whole community in which he is working. The description of different roles expected of instructor of adult learners are as follows.

Organiser of the Centre

As an organizer of the centre, the instructor has to (a) contract the prospective learners and leaders of the community, (b) Help the supervisor to conduct simple survey of the community, (c) Help to create a learning environment (d) Enroll illiterate adults to the centre (e) Motivate the dropouts to attend the centre and (f) Secure suitable place for running the centre in consultation with the learners local leaders etc.

Teacher of Literacy and Disseminator of Functional Information

As a teacher of literacy the instructor is expected to provide basic stimulus through a dialogue with the learners about their handicaps which reduce their self-confidence and lower their place within the status and power structure of the community. The instructor has to strive to promote reading, writing and computation skills among the learners in a specified period of time. He has to decide the timing of the Centre in consultation with the learners and take special classes for deserving adult learners to compensate the less of learning. Further, as disseminator of functional information, he should provide information to various occupational groups to improve their professional skills. A variety of information should be received and disseminated by the instructor.

Initiatior of Discussion and Awareness

The instructor has to understand what 'awareness' means in the context of the programme. He has to be well-informed about all important matters that relate to the life of the community e.g.., tenancy laws, land and labour laws, developmental schemes and loan facilities, health and extension services. It is the duty of the instructor to initiate discussion among the learners on varied topics and share their experiences, skills and knowledge with co-learners.

Organiser of Cultural and Recreational Programmes

The learners and other members of the community should be helped by the instructor to organize programmes of cultural and recreational activities like dramas, bajans, kirthans, games etc., which serve to enliven and enrich the life of the learners.

Mobilizer of Resources

The instructor has to mobilize the human and material resources required for the improvement of the functional skills of the learners and consequently their economic conditions. The instructor should arrange useful lectures by the experts in various fields and use local talents for the promotion of functional skills among adult learners. He should involve the educated youth and enlist support of Mahilamandals and youth clubs in running the centre.

Recorder of Educational Activities

The instructor should systematically note and record in a daily diary whatever they observe i.e., the problems he faces in carrying out his tasks, or the changes that he observes in the community. By writing about his experiences and ideas the instructor should be able to establish a flow of information from bottom to top.

Professional Devotion

As a professional devoter he should perform the following

things: (a) discuss about the better methods of instruction with co-instructors; (b) strive to gain expertise in instructing adult learners; (c) attend in-service training programmes; (d) seek advice from experts in adult education in solving professional problems; and (e) develop their knowledge by reading books, periodicals, newspapers etc.

Guidance

The instructor acts as guide to the adult learners. As a guide he should (a) assist the learners in solving their personal, social and academic problems, (b) assist the learners to develop study habits, (c) identify the slow learners and show special attention to their learning problems, (d) help the learners in getting benefits from the developmental programmes and so on.

When we look at various roles that have been idealized for instructor of adults any one can easily say that it is practically impossible for a poor instructor to perform so many roles (which are diversified and complicated) fully and satisfactorily. The objective in specifying so many roles seems to be; (a) firstly, to make the instructor be aware of the diversified roles he has to play to make the purpose of education a grand success; and (b) secondly, by being aware of the various roles he has to perform, the instructor is expected to do justice to the different roles assigned to him to the best of his ability. Of course, many things such as personality of the instructor, competencies possessed by the instructor and attitude of the instructor towards teaching etc. may effect in successful fulfilment of the different roles assigned to the instructor.

Extensive research studies have been conducted both in Indian and abroad on various aspects that effect the role-performance as well as role success of the school teachers. Researchers like Sorenson, Husek, and constance Yu (1963), Bledsoe, and Brown, (1968) have conducted studies on role expectations.

Bar and Others (1935), Ryans, D.G. (1951), Tom Arthur Lemake (1951), Hampton (1951), Peck, R.F. (1959), Freehill (1963), Gage (1965), Roger W. Oxford (1969), and Mala Kondaiah (1980) studied characteristics associated with effective teachers.

Studies by Saxena (1969), Kaul (1972), Tripathi (1972), Chhaya (1974), Goyal (1974), Srivastava (1974), Singh (1974), Gupta (1975),

Gupta (1977), illustrate the type of personality factors possessed by effective teachers.

Research findings of Adaval, (1952), Buch (1974), Debnath (1971), Deva (1966), Roy (1971), Bandey (1958) and others indicate possible factors commonly associated with teaching success of school teachers.

In the school, a teacher who has favourable attitude towards teaching will enjoy teaching. Studies in this area are Cook Heads and Calling (1951), Fox and Richey (1948), Leeds (1956), Lindgreen and Pattan (1958), Beamer and Ledbetter (1957), Ryans (1960), Rabinowitz and Travers (1955).

When we look for studies conducted on instructors of adult education on the above issues, not many studies are found. Some studies have been done in abroad on competencies to be attained by the adult educators. Studies by White (1950), Aker (1962), Madry (1963), Veri (1968), Niemi and Davison (1971), Fenn (1972), Ganeles (1974), Mocker (1974), Grabowski (1976) fall under this category.

In India, negligible studies have been conducted on various issues relating to adult education instructors and the field appears to be wide open. Many research studies that explore the various factors associated with effectiveness and role success of adult education instructors can be undertaken. The present study is an attempt in this direction.

2

Review of Related Literature

Right from the video times, teacher (instructor) is playing a significant role in the society. A teacher is supposed to play certain roles idealized by the society and is expected to discharge them skilfully with reference to educational activity in the society. With change of time, there is change in the type of roles the teacher is expected to perform.

The way the teacher discharges his roles is influenced by a number of factors such as his personality, environment, resources available, etc. An instructor working in adult education programme is expected to perform certain roles just as the formal school teacher is expected to discharge certain roles. The ultimate expectations from both i.e., formal school teacher and adult education instructor are more or less one and the same i.e., educationing their students effectively. The basic difference in their roles may be the type of approach they adopt i.e., the former deals with growing individuals and the latter with grown up individuals.

There are ample number of researches that have studied the various aspects of formal school teachers both in India and a broad. But, relatively few studies are done on instructors of adults and that too, a negligible extent in India. Though the studies on school teachers are not directly relevant to explain various issues relating to adult education instructors, still, they are relevant in the sense that they will provide an insight into the type of conclusions that may come out, if such studies are conducted on instructors of adult learners.

Some of the studies (which are relevant from the point of view of the present investigation) with provide clear background to the role-performance of instructors/teachers are presented below under various headings.

Firstly, studies which try to explore the characteristics that are possessed by effective teachers (which in turn influence their role-performance) are presented. Secondly, studies illustrating effective teachers personality (which in a way try to explain how role discharge by instructors is personality-oriented behaviour) are presented. Thirdly, studies indicating the attitude of teachers towards teaching (which in a way explain how effectively one discharges his roles) are presented. Fourthly, factors acting as catalysts to the success of teachers in teaching (which try to explain the intensity in discharging instructional roles of a teacher) are presented. Fifthly, some studies which specifically illustrate the competencies to be attained by adult educators are presented. Lastly, studies on teachers' role-performance which are directly relevant to the present study are presented.

Teacher Effectiveness and Related Studies

Meaning of the Term

Teaching is effective to the extent that the teacher acts in way that are favourable to the development of basic skills, understanding, work habits, desirable attitudes, value judgements and adequate personal adjustments of the pupils (Ryans, 1960).

Barr (1952) explains teacher effectiveness as a relationship between teachers, pupils and other persons concerned with the educational undertaking, all effected by limiting and facilitating aspects of the immediate situations.

Effectiveness is a degree to which an agent produces effects. Usually, these categories of effects in terms of the object effected are: a) pupil, b) school operation, and c) the school community (Remmers, 1952).

According to Dickson (1980), Teaching effectiveness is a demonstrated repertoire of competencies involved with 1) teaching plans and materials, 2) class-room procedures, 3) inter-personal skills, and

4) learners reinforcement-involvement reflected in teacher behaviour.

Gupta and Kapoor have derived the term "Teacher Effectiveness" as a repertoire of efficacy exhibited by a teacher in 1) instructional strategies, 2) class-room management, 3) personal disposition, temperament and tendencies, 4) evaluation and feed back, 5) interpersonal relations, 6) job involvement, 7) initiative and enthusiasm, 8) professional values, and 9) innovativeness respectively in the everyday teaching learning situation.

Studies on Teacher Effectiveness

Barr and Others (1935) employed some unique approaches to criterion development. Five criteria were employed: 1) gain in pupil achievement as measured by the Stanford Achievement Test, 2) a composite of scores on seven rating scales, 3) a composite of nine measures of qualities commonly associated with teaching success, 4) a composite of six tests of teaching ability chosen from composite three and 5) a composite of all nineteen variables combined variously.

Hampton (1951) employed ratings as the sole criterion of teacher effectiveness. For her study she has chosen twelve items as follows: 1) co-operation and loyalty, 2) knowledge of subject matter, 3) courtesy and friendliness, 4) interest in school activities, 5) discipline, 6) emotional poise, 7) general culture, 8) health and vitality, 9) personal appearance, 10) resourcefulness, 11) response to criticism and 12) speech.

Ryans (1951) undertook a study to investigate certain factors or conditions that might be related to effective teaching at the elementary school level and to estimate the extent to which measures of such conditions were associated with judgements of teaching effectiveness made by trained observers. The sample consisted of 275 women from 3rd and 4th grades and from 4 different communities.

The results of the study indicated that there was only one statistically significant difference between the teachers classified by school system in which they are employed. Amount of teaching experience seemed to be a factor of some importance as may be noted. No significant difference was noted between the groups of single and married teachers in any other criteria.

Lemake (1951) in his study, 'personality and teaching success' tried to determine whether there were characteristic personality differences between good and poor teachers. The criteria of teaching success were used in this study.

The results of the study indicated that good teachers were good for different reasons. It appeared that success may be a 'balance' and that to predict it one must understand what was required for the balance. It may be that on some such basis the accuracy of prediction may be improved.

Peck (1959) in his "predicting principal ratings of teacher performance from personality data" said that teacher personality is known to influence "teaching effectiveness". Freehill (1963) in his study of prediction of a teaching competence, found that the quality of teaching beyond the minimum if failure was related to ability, college entrance test, and academic success.

Gage (1965) questions why researchers continue to search for relationships between the teacher characteristics and pupil growth when their rewards were so meagre. According to him the review of literature at the present time allows for the selection of five global characteristics which seems to be components of effective teaching.

The five characteristics selected were; (i) warmth, (ii) cognitive organisation, (iii) orderliness, (iv) indirectness, and (v) problem solving abilities.

Malakondaiah (1980) studied characteristics of effective adult education instructors as viewed by adult education instructors. According to the study, the best characteristics were co-operation with learners capacity to organise programmes knowledge of subjects to be taught, and the ability to communicate the subjects. Sense of humour and ability to organise adult education centres were the least preferred ones.

Oxford (1969) in his study found certain ideal qualities attributed to adult education instructors. They were: 1) show of fairness, 2) sense of humour, 3) fond of knowledge, 4) good speaker-communicates well, 5) likes people-informal, 6) good organiser-uses lesson plans, 7) councils students, 8) good listener, 9) enthusiastic teacher, 10) varies methods of teaching, 11) careful observant, 12) knows students interests, 13) has neat appearance, 14) uses visual aids, 15) stimulates discussion, 16) raises questions, 17) knows sources of information, 18) considers individual differences, 19) relates well to students, 20) suggests further study, 21) has confidence in students, 22) is well prepared, 23) motivates learning, and 24) maintains interests in subject. The above qualities are generally considered as qualities possessed by effective instructors.

Personality Studies of Effective Teachers in India

Meaning of the Term

The word personality in simple terms means knowing of a person, that he is so-and-so and what he likes (Vermon, 1957). Vermon further adds- "while a man's intelligence, his bodily strength and skills are certainly parts of his personality, yet the term chiefly refers to his emotional and social qualities, together with the drives, sentiments and interests". Stagner (1961) is more concerned with the inner system of thought process of an individual and defines personality as "inner system of beliefs, expectancies, desires and values."

Eysenck (1953) defined personality as "More or less stable and enduring organization of persons character, temperament, intellect, and physique; which determines his unique adjustment to environment."

Personality is that which permits a prediction of what a person will do in a given situation. The goal of psychological research in personality is thus to establish laws about what different people will do in all kinds of social and general environmental situation. Personality is concerned with all the behaviour of the individual, both overt and under the skin (Cattell, 1950).

From the analysis of various definitions of personality by different psychologists, we notice that personality shows particular type of pattern which is composed of traits or specific qualities of behaviour which characterize the individual's unique adjustment to life as shown in his behaviour and thought. The "core" or centre of gravity of the personality pattern is the individuals concept of himself as person and related to the world in which he lives. The quality of his behaviour, expressed in the way he adjusts to people and things in his environment, is related to and, to a large extent determined by his self-concept.

There are good number of researches that have attempted to

study the nature of personality factors possessed by effective teachers. Some of the studies were as reported under.

Representative Studies

Saxena (1969) made an attempt to study the attitudes and personality of teachers. He used Cattell's 'Contact Personality Factors' (From 'A' Hindi version) on 139 teachers in U.P. in relation to their teaching competence. A coefficient of correlation of +. 60 with factor 'H' and +. 42 and +.36 with factors 'A' and 'H' respectively were obtained. With high teaching competence, these correlations were +.60, +0.6 and +.36 respectively, which shows a curvilinear relationship. It shows that a very high score on factor 'H' is typical of less competent teachers and only a moderately high 'H' is characteristic of a more successful teacher.

Kaul (1972) made a factorial study of certain personality variables of popular teachers in secondary schools. His objective was to differentiate the personality traits of popular and unpopular teachers. He used Cattell's 16 PF questionnaire. He came to the conclusion that the effectiveness of popular teachers was with respect to attitudes towards teaching, public examination results of their students and the appraisal of their work as teachers respectively.

Tripathi (1972) administered the 16 PF Test (From A) to 52 teacher-trainees and 52 experienced teachers to compare the personality profiles of working teachers and teacher trainees. The technique of profile matching was employed for smooth comparisons between the two groups. Only eight factors (A, E, F, G, I, L, N and Q_4) out of 16 personality factors distinguished the experienced teachers easily. These teachers were conscientious, persistent, sensitive, eliminate suspecting, Jealous, sophisticated and polished. The experienced teachers were significantly lower from the general population on factors A,E, F Q_4 and were aloof, stiff, submissive, soft hearted, plum and serious respectively.

Chhaya (1974) compared effective and ineffective teachers with respect to personality adjustment, teaching attitude and emotional stability. Eighty effective and 100 ineffective teachers were selected from 20 randomly selected schools of Kanpur district. Effectiveness and ineffectiveness were known on the basis of high school examination results (Board examinations of 1968, 1969 and 1970). She came to the conclusion that effective teachers had significantly better personality adjustment and favourable attitudes towards teaching. They were less interested in teaching than ineffective teachers, emotionally stable, more authoritarian and extrovert. She found that sex and age of a teacher were significantly related to his/her effectiveness.

Goyal (1974) studied some of the personality correlates of creativity in secondary school teachers under training. He was interested in knowing specially the personality differences in relation to sex and subject group as well as creativity differences in relation to sex and subject groups. He applied Cattell's 16 PF questionnaire and Torrance Tests of Creative Thinking as the tools. His sample consisted of 500 student teachers (200 male and 300 female) in the age range of 10 years to 47 years. He found that the personality differences between high and low creative student-teachers were very slight because highly creative persons did not enter teacher training colleges. Intelligence was found to be the most consistent personality correlate of creativity. Highly flexible student-teachers were more guilt prone and less imaginative. Highly creative females were having more self-conflict, were moralistic, socially precise and bold. Higher intelligence, emotional stability and tough mindedness were common personality traits found in science and mathematics groups at higher and lower levels of creativity.

Srivastava (1974) used 16 PF questionnaire (Cattell's Hindi version) on 52 pupil teachers and 52 experienced teachers to know the impact of professional experience on the modification of personality traits. He found that experienced teachers differed on factors A,E, F, H, Q_1, Q_2 and Q_3 from the pupil teachers.

Singh (1974) made a comparative study of the personality profiles of married and unmarried high school female teachers. She derived the personality profiles of these teachers with the help of Cattell's 16 PF questionnaire. The investigator found that the unmarried female teachers differed significantly on Factors A, F, L, O, Q_1 and Q_4 while the married teachers differed significantly on factors A, C, F, L and Q from the general population. Less scores on factors O and Q_4 were shown by the unmarried female teachers. Married female teachers were less stable and frustrated (C—). Female teachers (married or unmarried) were found to be significantly higher on factors L + and Q_1 +. It means that they are more suspicious and self-opinionated. These were significant on factors A and F from general population. Thus, they are reserved, critical, cool, detached, rigid and aloof respectively.

Gupta (1975) applied Cattell's 16 PF Test to predict teacher effectiveness through the use of a personality test. Three hundred male high school teachers having five to six years of teaching experience, 25 Principals and 350 students formed the sample. Other tools that were used were Teachers' Rating Scale and Pupils' Rating Scale respectively. The researcher noticed that highly effective teachers were more effectothymic (A+), more intelligent (B+), having more ego-strength (C+), more surgent (F+), more self-sentiment (Q_3+) and were less guilt prone, less suspicious (O—) in comparison to the general adult population. Less effective teachers were less intelligent (B—) with lower self-concept control (Q_3—) as compared to the general population. Highly effective teachers were significantly more intelligent (B+), emotionally stable (C+), assertive (E+), conscientious (G+), adventurous (H+), tender minded (I+), with higher self concept control Q_3+) and were more warm-hearted (A+) in comparison to the less effective teachers. The average effective teachers were more outgoing (A+), surgent and happy-go-lucky (F+), controlled and socially precise in comparison to the less effective teachers.

Gupta (1977) conducted a study regarding the personality structure of primary and upper primary school teachers. Eighty five teachers constituted the sample - the age range was 23 years to 38 years. Cattell's 16 PF Test was used. Means, S.D's were calculated for each factor in terms of stems and raw scores. The study showed that the primary school teachers are humble (E—), sober (F—), tender-minded (H—), forthright (N-—), and controlled (Q_3+1). Humbleness, tender-mindedness and forth righteousness are associated with submissiveness, day-dreaming and feminity, simple and unsophisticated nature. They have control over emotions and general behaviour. In fact the primary school teachers who are facing the bare necessities of daily life cannot help but be submissive, day-dreaming and unsophisticated in this materialistic age. It is not good for a teacher because he is supposed to be balanced from all sides.

Gupta (1977) performed a study on the personality characteristics, adjustment level, academic achievement and professional attitudes of successful teachers. The study intended to find out the personality traits of successful teachers and differentiate them from less successful teachers. It was found that teaching success was significantly related to the factors A, B, C, F, G, H, I, L, N, O, Q_3 and Q_4 of personality. The researcher also noticed that successful and less successful teachers were different in personality characteristics, adjustment and attitudes towards teaching. The personality factor as a group were better indicators of teaching success than individual factors.

Studies on Attitude of Teachers Towards Teaching

Attitudes generally refer to the inner feelings of a person. Attitude towards anything, is defined in different ways by different writers in different contexts.

Freeman (1962) defined attitude as 'a dispositional readiness to respond for certain situations, person or objects, in a constant manner which has been warned and has become one's typical mode of response'.

Teachers differ in their attitude towards teaching. An individual (teacher) who is having favourable or positive attitude towards teaching is supposed to be a more effective teacher than an individual who is having negative or unfavourable attitude. Good number of studies were conducted to estimate the effect of attitude of teachers towards teaching. Some of the studies reported below illustrate about this aspect.

In Cook, Leads and Calling (1951) through their investigations came to the conclusion that attitude of teachers towards children and school work can be measured with high reliability and that they are significantly related to teacher-pupil relations in the classroom.

Fox and Richey (1948) found variables of security, chance of advancement, good working conditions, pleasing environment, chances to serve society, work with young people, prestige, personal satisfaction, social contacts and other factors as advantages seen by prospective teachers. But, there were disadvantages, including low pay, restrict private life, poor working conditions, monotony, parental disapproval, responsibility, nerve strain, too many bosses, low-social standing, lack of prestige, lack of academic freedom, little tenure, politics and other factors mentioned by those of non-prospective teachers not intending to teach.

Leeds (1965) found that who get along well with pupils tend to be co-operative, friendly objective and emotionally stable, and to a lesser degree manifest sociability, social ascendancy, and masculinity in emotions and interests. Those who do not have high rapport with pupils tend to be critical and intolerant, hostile and belligerent, hypersensitive, depressed and emotionally unstable, and to a lesser degree tend toward submissiveness, shyness, seclusiveness and femininity.

Lindgreen and Pattan (1958) hypothesized that the attitudes of high school teachers are less favourable toward children and toward current educational theory and practice than are the attitudes of teachers in the lower grades.

Beamer and Ledbetter (1957) found that women teachers obtained a higher mean score of 76 compared to their men counterparts whose mean score was 61 on the MTAI. Similarly, in their investigation with a 50 item questionnaire, Lindgreen and Pattan (1958) reported that men teachers were and less favourably disposed to children and current educational theory and practice than women teachers.

In a very exacting study Ryans (1960) observed that at the elementary school level, men and women teachers differed in only four of the personal social characteristics studied. Men were less responsible and business like in class-room behaviour and more favourable towards democratic class-room practices, more inclined towards permissive, child-centered educational view points, and more emotionally stable than women. At the secondary school level, differences between the sexes were fairly general and pronounced with women tending to attain significantly higher scores on the seven scales measuring friendly, responsible stimulating class-room behaviour, favourable attitude towards pupils, democratic class-room practices, permissive educational view points and verbal understanding. Men teaches score significantly higher in emotional stability, however.

The limitations of conventional training programmes in modifying teacher attitudes were shown in the study of Rabinowitz and Travers (1955) that yielded evidence for improvement in the areas of pupil control, pupil-teacher tension, and mutual pupil teacher participation after training in a progressive programme but not in a conventional or conservative one. No differences between students and the two programmes were found before or during the training period.

Studies on Factors Affecting Teaching Success

Numerous attempts have been made to study the possible factors commonly associated with teaching success. There are good number of Indian studies.

Adaval (1952) in his study to find out the qualities of teachers under training, used a general knowledge test, an intelligence test and an aptitude test for teaching. The study revealed high correlation between intelligence and teaching aptitude. Debnathi, (1971) in his study of some important determinants of teaching efficiency, found that age, experience, academic achievement and training are significantly related to teaching efficiency. The coefficient of correlation between teaching efficiency and age, experience, academic achievement and training were +.21, +.24, +.24, +.19 and +.31 respectively.

Deva (1966) in his attempt to predict student teaching success used five predictor variables viz., intelligence, social adjustment, personality-adjustment, socio-economic status and academic achievement. He found the correlation between predictor variables and criterion measure to be significant. Personality was found to be the most important and intelligence the least important in predicting success in student teaching.

Pandey (1958) in constructing a teaching aptitude test, included the following variables: professional knowledge, vocabulary, number series, numerical reasoning, logical selection, general information and centroid method were 'general information and reading comprehension. Four factors derived through centroid method were "general educational factor, "reasoning" factor, "numerical skill" and "reading comprehension" factor.

Roy (1971) studied the relationship between teacher aptitude and teaching efficiency and found positive relationship between the two. Sherry constructed a predictive battery for success in teaching. The battery included the following tests: intelligence test, interest inventory, personality inventory and attitude scale. Intelligence was found to be the most important factor for success in teaching.

Studies on Competencies to be Attained by Adult Educators

Adult education professionals, have been concerned about the level of competence of those providing educational services to adults. Ganeles (1974) believes that "competence-based teacher education programmes for adult educators will provide better preparation than traditional programmes." Research ascertaining the competencies to be attained by adult educators has been conducted by several investigators.

White (1950) developed the following list of competencies which are appropriate for adult educators.

1. To gain a better understanding of the basic needs which cause adults to participate in educational programmes.
2. To gain a clear insight into the changing interests of adults in vocations, religion, family, leisure time activities, health and other areas of life.
3. To increase ability to apply psychological principles to the selection of objectives.
4. To acquire techniques for relating the programme more closely to the needs and interests of adults.
5. To acquire techniques for relating our programme more closely to the general needs of the community.
6. To become more skilful in recognizing community needs and resources that are important to adult education programmes.
7. To develop a better understanding of the kinds of educational methods most suitable for mature persons.
8. To develop a better understanding of the kinds of educational materials most suitable for mature persons.
9. To become familiar with procedures for 'keeping up' with new developments and material for adult education programmes.

Aker (1962) in his study identified 23 behaviours which were judged to be adequate criteria for determining the achievement of educational objectives. They were as follows:

1. Helps people control and adjust to change rather than maintain

the status quo.

2. Intelligently observes and listens to what is being said or done and uses this information is guiding his responses.
3. Selects and uses teaching methods, materials and resources that are appropriate in terms of what is to be learned and in terms of the needs and abilities of the individual learner.
4. Helps his clientele acquire the ability for critical thinking.
5. Provides an atmosphere where adults are free to search through trial-and-error without fear of institutional or interpersonal threat.
6. Identifies potential leaders and helps them to develop their potentials and capacities.
7. Makes use of existing values, beliefs, customs, and attitudes as a starting point for educational objectives.
8. Is actively involved in continuing study that will increase his professional competence.
9. Understands the role of adult education in society and is aware of the factors and forces that give rise to this function.
10. Activity shares, participates, and learns with the learners in the learning experiences.
11. Helps adults to actively set their goals, and provides a variety of means and opportunities for intensive-self evaluation.
12. Identifies and interprets trends that have implications for adult education.
13. Has clearly defined his unique role as an adult educator and understands his responsibility for performing it.
14. Arrange learning experiences so that learners can integrate theory and practice.
15. Is effective in building a teaching team among lay leaders and group members.
16. Uses the process of appraisal to evaluate programmes, and to help clarity and change objectives.

17. Is creative and imaginative in developing new programmes, and believes that innovation and experiment are necessary for the expansion of adult education.
18. Makes use of the contribution of all group members through the utilization of individual talents and abilities.
19. Works with schools, teachers, parents, and pre-adults to assist them in developing the motivation, attitudes, understanding, and skills necessary for lifelong learning.
20. Objectively presents contrasting points of view.
21. Assume the initiative in developing a strong national perception of importance and essentially of continuing education.
22. Recognizes when the communication process is not functioning adequately or when it breaks down.
23. Identifies, critically evaluates, and discusses scholarly work by investigators in adult education and related fields.
24. Madry (1963) distributed a questionnaire to directors of public school adult education programmes which contained 77 statements of functions, 33 competency statements and questions about problem areas. Competencies which were rated highest were basic understanding of programme organisation and administration, ability to establish wholesome relationships, and executive and supervisory ability. The major functions reported by respondents included:

    (1) organization and structure, (2) programme purpose, (3) programme planning and development, (4) instructional services and materials, (5) student personnel service, (6) staff personnel, (7) facilities and business management, (8) school community relations and promotion, (9) community services, (10) programme evaluation, and (11) research.

Adult educators who have doctorates were surveyed by Veri (1968) to assess their reaction to 60 learning total programme which would provide graduates with necessary competencies. The following list of 19 programme areas resulted from this survey. They were:

(1) history and philosophy of adult education; (2) designing and evaluating adult education programmes; (3) psychology of adult

education; (4) sociology of adult education; (5) social change; (6) special problems; (7) motivation; (8) organisation and administration of adult education; (9) methods and media in adult education; (10) educational psychology; (11) cultural change; (12) fundamental research techniques; (13) utilisation and evaluation of audio-visual aids; (14) public relations; (15) personnel administration; (16) internship in adult education to determine research needs and design a research project; (17) budget development and control in education; (18) public speaking; and (19) community planning and organisation.

A more concise list of competencies needed by an effective adult basic education teacher was developed by Fenn (1972) from a review of existing literature and suggestions of adult education leaders. A panel of experts from several areas of the country reviewed the list prior to ranking by selected adult basic education students, teachers, and administrators as well as professors of adult education.

The following were the ranks of 34 competency statements resulting from the study.

1. Skilfully uses a variety of appropriate adult teaching methods and techniques.
2. Knows the historical background of adult education and is aware of how his programme fits into it.
3. Is able to communicate effectively with adult students.
4. Has skill in guiding and counselling adult student.
5. Is actively involved in continuing study which will increase his professional competence.
6. Has knowledge of the financing of adult basic education.
7. Arranges learning experiences so that students can integrate theory and practice.
8. Believes that dialect is not bad English, but standard English is useful tool.
9. Understands the philosophical bases of adult education and has developed his own working (personal) philosophy.
10. Has knowledge and understanding of the economically disad-

vantaged and various ethic groups.

11. Helps students acquire the ability for critical thinking and problem solving.
12. Develops favourable public relations for the ABE programme.
13. Believes there is potentiality for growth in most people.
14. Is aware and works with agencies found within the community that can assist the students.
15. Selects and/or develops and uses materials appropriate to the needs and abilities of the individual.
16. Helps students, identifies needs and goals and provide meaningful feed back regarding progress towards these.
17. Has knowledge of economic and labour market information and relates it to the vocational endeavours of the students.
18. Makes use of contributions of all group members through the utilization of individual talents and abilities.
19. Helps students to control and adjust to change.
20. Believes that innovation and experimentation are desirable for the growth of adult education.
21. Secures active participation from students in the learning situation.
22. Locates, interprets and applies research findings to improve teaching and/or solve instructional problem.
23. Believes from freedom of thought and expression (open mind).
24. Understands the problems and principles of administration in adult education.
25. Has a thorough knowledge of adult psychology.
26. Understands the conditions under which adults are most likely to learn and applies that knowledge.
27. Diagnoses deficiencies in students basic skills.
28. Has knowledge and skill in the subject matter being taught (reading, writing, arithmetic).

29. Participates in professional organisations and/or associations of adult education.
30. Is skilful in writing behavioural objectives.
31. Functions effectively in a team teaching situation.
32. Provides for individualized instruction.
33. Has experience and skill in teaching children in elementary grades.
34. Is skilful in relating subject matter and content to the real life problems of the students.

Mocker (1974) identified 291 behaviours, attitudes and knowledge which should be exhibited by a competent adult basic education teacher. A nationally representative group of adult basic education teachers were requested to react to each of the 291 statements by indicating if a teacher of adult basic education requires no, slight, moderate, considerable, or complete competency in the activities cited in the statements. Inventory ratings were converted into a rank order list of all competencies into the following categories namely: scope and goal of adult education, curriculum, ABE learner; and instructional process. Each of these categories was separated into competencies related to knowledge, behaviour, and attitude within each of these subdivisions. Competencies were further separated into those of high priority and those of low priority.

Grabowski (1976) compiled a list of adult education competencies. The study resulted in the following descriptors of adult educators.

1. Understands and takes into account the motivational and participation patterns of adult learners.
2. Understands and provides for the needs of adults in learning.
3. Is versed in the theory and experiences in the practice of adult education.
4. Knows the community and its needs.
5. Knows how to use the various methods and techniques of instruction.
6. Possesses communication skills, including listening.

7. Knows where to locate and how to use educational materials.
8. Has an open mind and provides an atmosphere that allows adults to pursue their needs and interests.
9. Continues his own education
10. Is able to appraise and evaluate programmes.

Studies on Teachers Role—Performance

The teacher (instructor) is the central point of the whole educational programme by virtue of his creativity, imagination, resourcefulness, attitudes, values and behaviour direct teaching towards more desirable goals. They would know exactly what they have to do in a particular situation. An ideal teacher is a friend, philosopher and guide to his learners, and leader of the community. Some research studies were undertaken to understand the factors associated with role-performance of school teachers. Some of the representative studies are as follows.

Sorenson, Husek and Constance Yu (1963) through their study developed an instrument designed to assess teacher role expectations. A preliminary form administered to 284 students was designed to measure 6 role dimensions namely information giver, disciplinarian advisor, counselor, motivator and referrer. A factor analysis confirmed these 6 factors and provided a basis for a revised form which was administered to 94 students. The results also were factor analysed. On the basis for a revised form which was administered to 94 students. The results also were factor analysed. On the basis of the 2 studies, a revised set of key was developed for 5 of the 6 scales. Advisor and information giver scales were combined to form a single scale. Reliability estimates for the scales range from. 77 to .93. The scales have low to moderate inter-correlations.

Soles (1964) conducted a study on "Teacher Role Expectations and the Internal Organisation of Secondary Schools". The basic idea of the study was that some of the sources of role expectations, or pressures and demands upon individual personnel (teachers) in the small work unit (class-room) may be rooted in the particular type of structural arrangement of the organisation (school). In this study teacher role expectations were regarded as dependent variables within the organisational structure of the schools.

The terms "role expectations" and "internal organisation" were basic analytic tools in the above study. The measure of teacher role expectations used was an adaptation of the Valenti-Nelson (1951) Survey of Teaching Practices which consists of 102 paired comparison statements dealing with a variety of situations which teachers encounter in the teaching role. Built into the instrument were 17 different issues such as: Handling minor disciplinary problems, dealing with individual differences, planning classroom work, motivating pupils, dealing with people cliques, and dealing with students organisations. There are four alternative methods of handling each of these issues. Each alternative is consistent with one of the four models. Role A-impersonal, Role B-Self-sufficient, Role C-counselling, Role D-Group Development.

The results of the study indicated firstly that the teachers from multiple period type schools did emphasize the group development role expectations. Secondly, teachers in the single-period curriculum scheduling schools did have significantly higher mean staff scores on the technical self-sufficient direction. Thirdly no significant differences were found between staff role scores from the multiple- and single period type schools for either the impersonal-bureaucratic (Role-A) or the counselling guidance (Role-C).

Bledsoe, and Brown (1968) conducted study on "Role perception of secondary teachers as related to pupils perceptions of teacher behavioural characteristics." In the study the Role expectations of 178 Georgia secondary teachers was measured by TPQ (Teacher Practice Questionnaire). Pupils perceptions was measured by pupil observation survey (POSR), and pupils attitudes were analysed by sex, age, experience, perception, field, grade level, and selected interaction efforts.

The results drawn from the study were: Science and mathematics teachers perceived the advice information giver role more important than did social studies teachers. Age and sex differentially influenced the teachers perception of the motivator role. For the disciplinarian role, grade level and the interaction effect of sex by field were significant.

The foregoing brief report of studies highlight that very large number of factors influence school teachers and their teaching behaviour. Some of these factors are organismic in that they refer to the individual while others pertain to the nature of the task and conditions of the task they have to perform.

The review indicates that there is much scope and need to investigate the effect of individualistic factors and task factors on adult education instructor's effectiveness. Of these, studies on personality factors associated with effective adult education instructors, role-performance and factors effecting role success of adult education instructors are much warranted. Research on these factors is expected to throw better light to understand and review adult education instructor in right perspective.

3

Statement of the Problem, Objectives, Hypotheses and Method of Study

Statement of the Problem

A brief review of related literature indicates that several studies have been conducted to study the characteristics, personality etc. of successful teachers in the formal school system. But, relatively few studies have been conducted to assess various problem that come in the way of successful discharging of various roles assigned to teachers. This is more so with reference to the problems that come in the way of successful role functioning of instructors' working under National Adult Education Programme (NAEP).

Problem

The instructor working in adult education centre is expected to play many roles. They have instructional responsibilities, counselling responsibilities, public relations responsibilities and many others as well. As already indicated, in recent years, the instructional role of an instructor has changed from a dispenser of information to that of an instructional manager. As an instructional manager the instructor has the responsibility for creating an environment where learning can take place. In this role, the instructor has to determine learning objectives, diagnose learners problems, plan learning activities, implement the programme and evaluate learner's progress.

Various major roles the instructor has to play are identified and spelt out in the hand book "training of Adult Education functionaries" published by the directorate of Adult Education, Ministry of Education and Social Welfare, Government of India, New Delhi. They are : organizer of the Centre, Teacher of Literacy and disseminator of functional information, Initiator of Discussion and Awareness, Organizer of Cultural and recreational Programmes, mobilizer of resources, recorder of educational activities, professional devotion and guidance.

The diversity of roles listed above appear to be quite ambitious when considered in terms of the qualifications and honorarium paid to the instructors. In order to be successful in performing his roles, the instructor has to shoulder many responsibilities, adopt to many situations, and exercise leadership under multitude of circumstances. This means, instructors should have strong will and at the same time adoptability to a variety of conditions. The adult education instructors with their background may find if difficult to perform the various roles expected of them in an ideal way. Gaps are certain to exist between the achieved and expected role performance of the instructors.

Objectives of the Study

Based on the above illustration, the objectives of the study were:

1) to estimate the amount of discrepancy that exist between idealized performance of each role assigned to the instructor and that discharged in actual practice;

2) to know the reasons that cause discrepancy in successful discharge of each role assigned to the instructors; and

3) to study the amount of discrepancy that exists in actual performance of roles from the ideology due to education, sex and caste differences.

Hypotheses

Based on the problem the following hypotheses were framed for testing.

Major Hypotheses

The subjects of the sample does not deviate significantly from the ideology of various roles assigned to them in actual discharge due to education, sex or caste differences.

In the light of the major hypothesis, the following sub-hypotheses were framed.

1) Subjects of the sample does not deviate significantly from the ideology of 'organizers of the centres' role assigned in actual discharge due to education, sex or caste differences.

2) Subjects of the sample does not deviate significantly from the ideology of 'teachers of literacy and disseminators of functional information', role assigned in actual discharge due to education, sex or caste differences.

3) Subjects of the sample does not deviate significantly from the ideology of 'initiators of discussion and awareness" role assigned in actual discharge due to education, sex or caste differences.

4) Subjects of the sample does not deviate significantly from the ideology of 'organizers of cultural and recreational programmes' role assigned in actual discharge due to education, sex, or caste differences.

5) Subjects of the sample does not deviate significantly from the ideology of 'mobilizers of resources' role assigned in actual discharge due to education, sex or caste differences.

6) Subjects of the sample does not deviate significantly from the ideology of 'recorders of educational activities' role assigned in actual discharge due to education, sex or caste differences.

7) Subjects of the sample does not deviate significantly from the ideology of 'devoters to profession' role assigned in actual discharge due to education, sex or caste differences.

8) Subjects of the sample does not deviate significantly from the ideology of 'guidance' role assigned in actual discharge due to education, sex or caste differences.

Construction of the Questionnaire

For the purpose of testing the hypothesis framed a questionnaire was necessary to estimate the discrepancy existing between roles idealized for instructors and the amount of successful discharge of various roles by the instructors in actual practice. As there was no standardised questionnaire readily available for use, the investigator has to develop a questionnaire of his own.

Firstly, various major roles that were supposed to be performed by the instructor were drawn keeping the instructor manual "Training of Adult Education Functionaries" as a guide. Under each main role, the various sub-roles supposed to be performed by the instructor were listed out. The entire list was given to 25 supervisors and 25 instructors, who were all educated (graduates) and were asked to comment and give their suggestions. Based on their suggestions, various roles identified were arranged under eight major heads. The eight major heads identified were:

1. organizer of the centre;
2. teacher of literacy and disseminator of functional information;
3. initiator of discussion and awareness;
4. organizer of cultural and recreational programme;
5. mobilizer of resources;
6. recorder of educational activities;
7. professional devotion; and
8. guidance.

In all, 62 roles were identified which an instructor has to discharge. Against each role four gradations were given namely Easy to perform/Moderately easy to perform/Performed with difficulty/ and not possible to perform. They had the scores 4,3,2 and 1 respectively. The instructors were asked to read out each statement (role) and indicate how far that particular role can be performed by the instructor keeping in view the four gradations.

For all the roles, a common question namely 'indicate the problems if any in discharging the role' was asked. Space was provided in the questionnaires for listing out the problems by the instructors under each role. The questionnaire was in Telugu and it was administered to instructors in batches of 15 to 20 numbers at a time.

Brief Plan of the Study

Subject of the Study

For the purpose of the present investigation National Adult Education Programme (NAEP) instructors who have completed or about to complete their term as instructors, representing caste groups, sex groups, and education group were required. On the whole, for the purpose of the present study a sample of 240 instructors representing caste, sex, and education groups were randomly chosen from the lists of instructors working in Sri Kalahasti and Naidupet projects, Chittoor district, Andhra Pradesh. In choosing the sample, firstly, combined lists of instructor's of both the projects representing scheduled castes on one side and other castes on the other side were drawn. From each caste list 30 males who had education above 10th class and 30 males who had education below 10th class were chosen. Similarly, from each caste list 30 female instructors who had educational qualification above 10th class and 30 female instructors who had below 10th class qualification were chosen.

The details of the sample graphically represented were as follows :

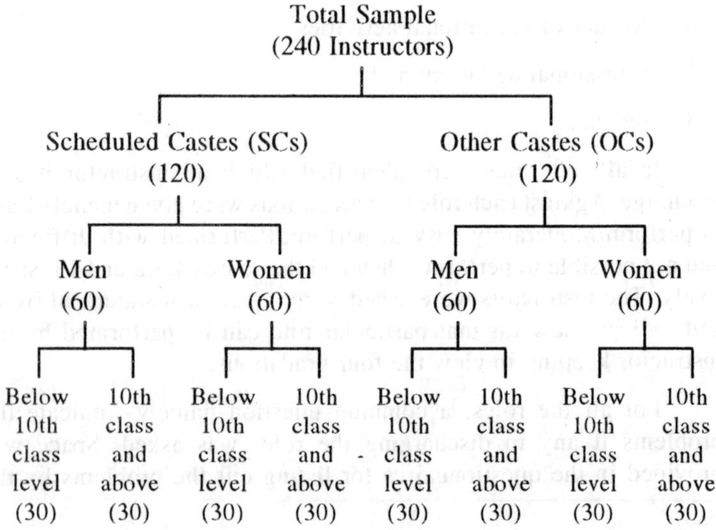

Method of Study

The answers given by instructors for each role were tabulated taking the scores given to the gradation against each role. The discrepancy for each role was calculated in terms of percentages. To know the discrepancy in discharge of each major role and roles as a whole with reference to education, sex and caste, the analysis of variance was carried out. Wherever the values are significant to know further significance within each education, sex or caste group, the Duncan's test was carried out. The results thus obtained were discussed in the coming chapters.

4
Results and Discussion

As already indicated, the objectives of the study were:

(a) to estimate the amount of discrepancy that exist between idealized performance of each role assigned to the instructor and that discharged in actual practice;

(b) to know the reasons that cause discrepancy in the successful discharge of each role assigned to the instructors;

(c) to study the amount of discrepancy that exist in actual performance of roles from the ideology due to education, sex, and caste differences.

Keeping the above objectives of the study in view, the results of the investigation are presented in two parts. Part-I of the results pertain to the first two of the above mentioned objectives viz. estimation of discrepancy in performance of roles and reasons causing such discrepancy. Part-II of the results pertain to the comparison of role performance by instructors with reference to education, sex and caste. In Part-I of the study only simple statistical techniques were used. Firstly, mean performance level of all the instructors in general for each role were calculated. Then, the discrepancy that exists in the mean performance for each role from that of idealized one was calculated. Based on the amount of discrepancy, the percentage of discrepancy in the performance of each role by the instructors was also calculated. All those details explaining mean amount of discrepancy, and the percentage of discrepancy were shown in the form of tables for each of the roles performed by the instructors under various headings and the details were discussed.

In Part II of the study statistics widely used were analysis of variance and Duncan's new multiple range test. In this part of the study, three way analysis of variance was done for each of the sub-group roles of the instructors as well as to instructors roles as a whole, taking education, sex and caste as factors. There were eight sub-group roles chosen for the instructors. They were:

(a) organizer of the centre; (b) Teacher of literacy and disseminator of functional information; (c) Initiator of Discussion and Awareness; (d) Organizer of cultural and recreational programmes; (e) Mobilizer of resources; (f) Recorder of educational activities; (g) Professional devotion; and h) Guidance.

Analysis of variance (F-Test) was adapted to this study based on the assumption of normality of distribution and homogeneity of variance of the distributions that were compared. It was presumed that the data obtained in this investigation confirmed to this requirements. In fact, the F-test is a robest test that is relatively insensitive to violations of the assumptions of the normality of distribution and homogeneity of variance (Edward, 1968).

In the present investigation wherever the analysis of variance (F-test) was employed, the Ns of the comparison groups were equal. Analysis of variance was therefore carried out straight away without applying the test of normality and the homogeneity of variance.

Based on the results the analysis of variance wherever significant interactions were found for such cases Duncan's new multiple range test was applied. This additional testing was necessary because, through analysis of variance one can know only how far the set of means chosen differ significantly. This alone is not satisfactory. One would like to know how the means differ. Is every mean significantly different from every other? Are there significant differences between some of the means and not between others? If one wishes to determine which of the differences between the chosen means are significant, and which are not- the suggested procedure is Duncan's new multiple range test. The test procedures are quite useful whenever one is concerned with multiple comparisons among the means. Keeping this in view for further analysis of the present test results the Duncan's new multiple range test was adapted.

PART—I

ESTIMATION OF DISCREPANCY IN THE PERFORMANCE OF INSTRUCTOR ROLES AND THE REASONS CAUSING SUCH DISCREPANCIES

In this part of the study as already indicated the discrepancy that exists in actual performance of the roles by the instructors in comparison to the idealized performance of the roles was discussed under eight major roles identified for the purpose.

They were: 1) organizer of the centre, 2) Teacher of Literacy and disseminator of functional Information, 3) Initiator of Discussion and Awareness, 4) Organizer of cultural recreational programmes, 5) Mobilizer of Resources, 6) Recorder of Educational Activities, 7) Professional Devotion and 8) Guidance.

The discrepancy that exists in the performance of each sub-role chosen under the major role and the reasons for such discrepancy if any with reference to the particular roles were discussed in detail in appropriate places. Finally, at the end, the overall estimation was done with reference to the overall discrepancy of the instructor role taking into account the major roles identified for the purpose of the study were as follows.

1. ORGANIZER OF THE CENTRE

Instructor of an Adult Education Centre should be a competent person to carry on the tasks of educating the adult learners successfully. Competency of an instructor may by interpreted in terms of his ability, power, skill, knowledge etc. in discharging different roles assigned to him. One of the major roles which stand as a testimony to the competency of an adult education instructor is his capacity in organizing the centre successfully throughout the programme period. The various roles identified to judge the potentiality of the instructor in organising the Centre according the present study were as given below:

1) Constitute a local advisory committee for adult education centre.
2) Motivate the drop-outs to attend the centre.

3) Assist agencies and organizations undertaking community development programmes.

4) Promote learning environment in the adult education centre.

5) Collect materials like slates, books, and hurricane lamps from the Project officer.

6) Convince prospective learners to attend adult education centre.

7) Explain about NAEP and its objectives to the adult learners.

8) Assist the Supervisor in surveying the community needs and facilities in running the adult education centre.

9) enroll illiterate adults to the centre.

In ideal conditions, an instructor is expected or able to discharge all the above roles successfully at cent percent level. But, ideology as it is well known to be always deviates from actual practice of things. It is true with reference to the level of performance of different roles by the instructors of the present study in their capacity of organization of the centres.

The various sub-roles that are identified under the major heading 'organizer of the centre', mean performance of the instructors on each role, level of discrepancy from the ideology (considering 4 points score as cent percent) and percentage of discrepancy are presented in Table 4.1 in hierarchical order starting from the high discrepancy mean and ending with the low discrepancy mean.

As a front line worker of National Adult Education Programme (NAEP), to start with the instructor has to motivate and convince the prospective learners to attend the adult education centre. The phrase prospective learners are generally mean (as per NAEP guidelines) adult men and women who are illiterate and who are in 15-35 years age group. Many people at this age will have settlement in life in some job or other and be earning their own livelihood.

Such people generally will not have belief and confidence in adult education programme in the sense that the programme is going to be of some help to them in some form or other for their betterment if they spend their time and energy for its sake at their late age. They may pose number of questions and answers to some of them may be a tough job on the part of the instructor. But well trained instructor

Table 4.1 : Instructors Mean Performance and Discrepancy Scores and Percentage of Discrepancy for Each Sub-Role of the Major Role 'Organizer of the Centre'

S. No.	S.No. of the Role in Question-naire	*Description of the Role*	*Mean* Score Points*	*Discre-pancy Points*	*Percentage of Discre-pancy*
1	4	Constitute a local advisory committee for adult education centre	3.26	0.74	22.70
2	7	Motivate the Drop-outs to attend the centre.	3.30	0.70	21.21
3	9	Assist agencies and organizations undertaking community development programmes.	3.51	0.49	13.96
4	6	Promote learning environment in the adult education centre.	3.52	0.48	13.64
5	8	Collect materials like slates, books, and harican lamps from the project officer.	3.56	0.44	12.36
6	1	Convince prospective learners to attend adult education centre.	3.60	0.40	11.11
7	3	Explain about NAEP and its objectives of the adult learners.	3.70	0.30	8.11
8	2	Assist the Supervisor in surveying the community needs and facilities in running the adult education.	3.71	0.29	7.82
9	5	Enroll illiterate adults to the centre.	3.78	0.22	5.82
		Scores on the Major Role as a whole	3.55	0.45	12.68

Note : 240 Adult Education Instructors Represented the Sample of the Study.

* : Maximum Possible Score = 4 Points.

using his common sense may be able to clarify many of their doubts and convince them to attend the centre which is going to thrive for a period of.10 months. As per item No. 6 of Table 4.1, the instructors of the present study seem to be good enough in convincing the prospective learners to attend the centres as there is only 11.11 per cent laps on their part in discharging this duty. In other words there is nearly 90 per cent success in performance of the role by them.

The marginal failure in the performance of this role by the instructors is generally attributed to two factors. Firstly, there were a set of learners who refuse to attend the centres in the absence of immediate monetary benefits. Secondly, some of the learners were practically unable to attend the centers as they find it hard to have spare time to attend adult education programmes.

It is not enough if the instructor simply convinces the adult learners to attend the centre. He must take all possible steps for their enrolment in the centre and make them morally bound to attend the centre. Once enrolment is there, the instructor can have some grip over them and can constantly check their attendance in the centre. He should see that at least 30 enthusiastic and self-motivated learners are enrolled in the centre run by him. The instructors of the sample appear to be quite good in this tasks as there is only negligible gap (about 6%) in performance of this particular role. Practically the instructors does not pose any problems in enrolment of illiterate adults in literacy centres.

Once the learners are convinced about the importance of adult education centre and enrolled in it, it is the responsibility of the instructor to see that proper learning environment is provided in the centre. Learning environment means provision of proper physical facilities like ventilation, lighting and sitting arrangements, making the learning activity as informal as possible so that the learners will learn at ease without tension and disheartening. More novelty in the method of teaching adopted by the instructor, better will be the encouragement for fruitful learning activity. The instructors of the present study appear to be fairly good in providing proper learning environment.

There is only a marginal failure (about 14%) in performance of this role according to them. This much failure is quite natural as generally there will be set back to learning environment some time or other however careful the instructor may be.

Some of the problems identified as hindrance to the performance of this role are: lack of proper place to run the centre at various seasons, lack of proper lighting facilities at some places etc.

The learners who are enrolled in the centres, after attending sometime, may again get many doubts about the utility of the programme for their present and future day today life activities. At this junction one of the ways to convince the learners is by explaining to them about the vast planning and objectives of national adult education programme and how it is really going to help the masses in general. Once the instructor begins to say that the government is not unwise in spending so much money on this programme if it is really going to be a waste and asks the learners to think logically about it, probably, they will be convinced about the importance of participating in NAEP which in turn motivates the adult learners to attend the centres regularly with confidence on future benefits.

The instructors of the present study are almost successful in convincing the adult learners about the importance of NAEP. By and large the instructors have not faced any problems in explaining about the objectives and importance of NAEP to adult learners.

Adult learners who are attending the centre are generally people having their own occupations and routine activities. Many of them have to adjust their timing in order to attend the centre. Inspite of their effort to attend the centre regularly, sometimes, they feel disheartedwith the problems they have to face which in turn may dilute their motivation in attending the centre. Whenever an adult is not attending the centre continuously for a period of 3 or 4 days, the instructor should take note of such learners. He should visit the learners and try to find out what are the problems actually faced by them and try to provide solutions of their problems which are coming in the way of attending the centre to the best of his ability. He should also console and provide due comfort to them by explaining the fact that problems always will be there and one has to find ways and means of overcoming them to the best of is ability. By such type of talk and persuasion, the learners who are temporary dropouts will generally be motivated to attend the centre again leaving aside their personal problems that come in the way of attending the centre. The instructors of the present study appear to be performing this role at a fairly satisfactory level (70%).

The reasons for the discrepancy (about 21%) as illustrated by the instructors are as follows. Firstly, the instructors feel that it is very ambitious role which is performed by the instructors for the meagre payment they are getting. Many of them feel that an instructor can do his best for the sake of learners during the time allotted for running the centre. But, they can not go on spending their time all the way closely watching and guiding all the learners attending the centres. In a way they feel that it is practically not possible also, even if the instructor is interested in doing so.

As organiser of the centre another important function to be performed by the instructor is: to collect reading materials like books, charts, posters, etc., writing materials like slates and slate pencils; physical amenities like black-board, hurricane lamps, etc.; from the project officer. He should collect material necessary quite promptly as and when the stocks are received by the project officer. He should also be careful about the kerosine stock and the way of functioning hurricane lamps well in advance so that they will not become hindrances to regular running of the centre. The instructors of the sample to be performing this activity fairly well to the best of their ability. The marginal discrepancy of about 12 per cent noted in performance of this role is attributed to the lapses on the part of the project authorities to supply certain of the materials in time.

The duty of the instructor as an organizer of the centre will not stop by simply looking at the learners and their attendance at the centre and by procuring materials from the project authorities. He should see that the centre runs more efficiently on the advice of local talents who can point out the lacuna in running the centre and ways and means of overcoming them. For this purpose constitution of a local advisory committee will be of great help. The instructors of the sample appear to be performing this role to a satisfactory level though not excellently.

The reasons for their 22.7 per cent discrepancy in performance of the role is attributed by some to the non-co-operative attitude of the local leaders and by some to less interest shown by the members selected to the committee in attending the meetings of the Committee.

The instructor can understand the needs of the community in a better way and can function harmoniously with them if he has survey details about the community needs with him. The Supervisor of the centres will be doing the community needs survey before starting the centre in any village. Assisting the supervisor in such duties is one of the roles to be performed by the instructors. By doing so, the instructor is not only discharging this role but he is getting a comprehensive idea about the communication which he is working. All the instructors of the sample appear to be quite good in performing this role and as there is only negligible discrepancy (7.82%) in their discharge of this role.

There are many agencies working for the welfare and progress of the weaker sections. Many community development programmes are undertaken for the benefit of weaker sections. Most of the learners attending the centres generally belong to the weaker-sections. So, the instructor by assisting agencies undertaking community development programmes will in a way, be assisting his own adult learners coming to the centre. More he assists such agencies better will be the respect and regard to instructors from the adult learners. It provides a type of faith in them and encourages them indirectly to attend the centre regularly.

On the whole the instructors of the sample appear to have nearly 87 per cent success in discharge of this major role 'organiser of the centre'. They appear to have done to the best of their ability in constituting a local advisory committee for adult education centre, motivating the dropouts, assisting agencies undertaking community development programmes, promoting learning environment in the centre, collecting necessary material for learning activity, and convincing the learners to attend the centres. In addition, they seems to be fairly good in explaining about NAEP and its objectives to adult learners and in assisting the supervisor in surveying the community needs.

2. TEACHER OF LITERACY AND DISSEMINATOR OF FUNCTIONAL INFORMATION

Teaching is considered as one of the noblest professions. Right from the ancient times, the teacher or instructor whether he is working in formal school system or in Adult Education programme, is expected to possess specialized knowledge in his area and should follow certain ethical standards. Basically, the teacher/instructor is expected to possess competency to carry out the task of educating his students successfully. When we look at this basic requirement from the point of view of adult education instructor, we look for his efficiency in terms of the amount of literacy skills gained by adult learners and the amount of functional information they are able to receive. Certain roles which judge the quality of the instructor as teacher of literacy and disseminator of functional information identified in this study are as follows.

1. Use instructional material like charts, posters, etc. effectively.
2. Provide relevant information to various occupational groups to improve their professional skills.
3. Conduct special classes for deserving adult learners to compensate the loss of attendance in the centre.
4. Pay special attention to the learning needs of weaker sections who suffer from multiple disadvantages.
5. Identify adult learners needs and select instructional content for the course.
6. Fix timings of running the center in consultation with the learners.
7. Impart literacy skills-reading, writing and arithmetic to adult learners.
8. Provide learning units that stimulate the learners to participate actively in the learning process.
9. Use chalk-board effectively to illustrate the content of the lesson.

In ideal conditions, an instructor will be able to discharge all the above roles successfully to the fullest extent. But in actual practice there always exists a gap between ideal performance and actual performance. It is quite true with reference to the level of performance of different roles by the instructors of the present study in the capacity as Teacher of literacy and disseminator of functional information.

The various sub-role that are identified under the major heading 'Teacher of literacy and disseminator of functional information; mean performance of the instructors on each of this role, level of discrepancy (from the ideology), and percentage of discrepancy are presented in Table 4.2 in hierarchical order starting from the high discrepancy mean and ending with the low discrepancy mean.

Table 4.2 : Instructors Mean Performance and Discrepancy Scores and Percentage of Discrepancy for Each Sub-Role of the Major Role 'Teacher of Literacy and Disseminator of Functional Information'

S. No.	*S.No. of the Role in Question-naire*	*Description of the Role*	*Mean* Score Points*	*Discre-pancy Points*	*Percentage of Discre-pancy*
1	13	Use instructional material like charts, posters etc. effectively	2.55	1.45	56.86
2	17	Provide relevant information to various occupational groups to improve their professional skills.	2.86	1.14	39.86
3	16	Conduct special classes for deserving adult learners to compensate the loss of attendance in the centre.	2.98	1.02	34.23
4	18	Pay special attention to the learning needs of weaker sections who suffer from multiple disadvantages.	3.39	0.61	17.99
5	10	Identify adult learners needs and select instructional content for the course.	3.53	0.47	13.31
6	12	Fix timings of running the centre in consultation with the learners.	3.67	0.33	8.99
7	11	Impart literacy skills-reading writing and arithmatic to adult.	3.70	0.30	8.11
8	15	Provide learning units that stimulate the learners to participate actively in the learning process.	3.71	0.29	7.82
9	14	Use chalk-board effectively in illustrate the content of the lesson.	3.82	0.18	4.71
		Scores on the Major Role as a whole	3.36	0.64	19.05

Note : 240 Adult Education Instructors Represented the Sample of the Study.

* : Maximum Possible Score = 4 Points.

As a teacher of literacy, a competent instructor can be described as a person whose instruction results in increasing the adult learners literacy skills. Literacy skills means (as per NAEP guidelines) reading simple sentences and to write them in their own and to work out or calculate simple arithmetic in their own. The learners should be able to read newspapers instructions, signboards, and information relating to their work and activities in their daily life. The programme lays emphasis on literacy because literacy is the basic tool, and that literacy should be relevant to learner's life. So, the instructor should have the competency of integrating these literacy skills (reading writing and arithmetic) with functional knowledge to get better result that is, prospecting the adult learners in the acquisition and utilization of literacy skills. As per item No. 7 of Table 4.2, the instructors of the study seem to be good in imparting literacy skills-reading, writing and arithmetic to adult learners and there is only 8.11 per cent laps on their part in discharging this function. It seems that there is 92 percent success in performance of this role and no specific problems were expressed by the instructors in the performance of this role when they were asked for the same.

Chalk-board is one of the low cost aid that is invariably present in all the adult education centres. The instructor should use it as effectively as possible in teaching the 3 R's to the adult learners. The learners can better understand and identify the ways and means of writing alphabets, words and sentences written on the board by the instructor for the purpose arithmetic problems like additions, subtractions, divisions can be better illustrated only through effective use of chalk board. As can be seen from Table 4.2 (Vide item No. 9), all the instructors seem to perform this function extremely well in comparison to other sub-roles. The discrepancy percentage noted for this role which is below 5 per cent is almost negligible. Since there is almost near perfection in performing this role, the instructors have not posed any problems in discharge of this role which is quite natural.

In addition to the chalk-board, to supplement illustration of the content of the lessons, the instructor should make use of instructional material like charts, posters etc. Effectively that are at his disposal. The learners will have concrete idea about the details of certain things when they are illustrated through charts of posters than merely imagining about them. For example, if there is a lesson on road signs and how to understand their meaning, the lesson will be better understood if the illustration is followed using a sign board chart. The instructors of the present study are less effective (lowest performed sub-role) in discharging this role as there is not even 50 percent success by them in use of charters and posters to supplement their teaching.

Two reasons are attributed as draw-backs in performance of this role. Firstly, there is no proper supply of relevant charts and posters (that can supplement the lesson contents) from the project management. Secondly, the instructors were neither technically nor financially sound to prepare or procure charts and posters that will be of use in their instructional programme.

The adult learners who attend the adult education centres generally attend the centres keeping in mind certain of their needs. Though, the instructor has limited choice in selecting the instructional content based on the needs of adult learners coming under is purview, yet he can make some efforts in selecting an reorganizing the material with slight modifications here and there (without deviating from the normal track) to meet the needs of adult learners as far as possible. For instance, functional information may be of various kinds. But, the instructor has to choose information to be disseminated to the adult learners based on the occupation of the majority of learners attending to his centre. The instructors of the sample can be considered good at this function as there is only about 13 per cent discrepancy from the idealized condition. The marginal failure in performance of the role may be due to diversity of the needs felt by the adult learners. Satisfaction of all is practically impossible for any instructor.

The instructor should divide the course content logically into different learning units to be covered at a specific time. He should always start with the most familiar learning unit so that the learners will be at ease and will be motivated to learn with confidence. This confidence will stimulate the learners to participate in the learning process effectively. The skill of the instructor can be seen in promoting such stimulating confidence among the adult learners while presenting the learning units. The instructors seem to be very good in this skill as there is only about 8 per cent discrepancy in actual practice of this role when compared with ideology.

According to instructors of the sample, even this slight discrepancy can be covered if proper instructional aids like charts, posters etc. which can attract the attention of adult learners are provided to them.

The instructor apart from teaching literacy skills should also provide relevant information to various occupational groups to improve their professional knowledge and skills. For example, to a group of adult learners who's main occupation is agriculture, the instructor can provide information to them about high yielding varieties, cash crops, discriminate use of manures at right time to a right crop, method of getting crop loans from banks etc. There is wide discrepancy (about 40%) in the performance of this role by the instructors can be seen from item 2 of Table 4.2. The wide discrepancy may be due to various facts. Firstly, the instructors working under the adult education programme are not having sufficient background knowledge to pass on functional information to the fullest extent successfully based on their clientele group. Secondly, many of the instructors were not trained properly about the method of disseminating functional information. Lastly, the general standard of their educational level is also responsible for their ignorance about certain of the aspects relating to functional information that is needed by adult learners.

It is not enough if the instructors teaches 3 R's and disseminates functional information to adult learners who attend the centres regularly. Some of the learners though very much interested in attending the centre/centres may fail to do so due to various problems or preoccupations in their day-to-day life activities. Overcoming of them may be practically impossible on certain occasions. For such type of learners, the instructors should conduct special classes to cover the units missed by them during their absence from the centre. Such an activity not only helps the occasional dropouts, but also gives them a type of confidence in the instructor—that he is striving hard for their betterment and prosperity. The instructors of the sample appear to be performing this activity to a barely satisfactory level. Yet, the discrepancy in performance of the role in contrast to its ideology is as wide as 34 per cent. So, there is need for special attention in performance of this role by the instructors.

Another factor which the instructor has to take care of is, paying special attention to weaker-sections who suffer from multiple disadvantages. Though the government has introduced many schemes and programmes for the benefit and uplift of people belong to the weaker sections, many of them are not reaching them properly. Some of the reasons attributed to this are, their illiteracy, ignorance and lack of proper communicative channels which enlighten them about the developmental programmes at their disposal. The instructor can play a significant role in this regard by acting as a liaison and helping the people belonging to weaker-sections to receive the fruits of the developmental programmes. The instructors of the present study appear to be discharging this role quite well as there is about 82 percent success in performance of this role.

The common problems expressed by the instructors with reference to the above two roles is lack of additional time for devotion to the type of adult learners as described above. Some of the instructors also feel that it is too much expectation from them in this regard when the meagre salaries paid to them is taken into account.

The success of any instructor as Teacher of Literacy and Disseminator of Functional information is considerably effected by the timings in which he is running the centre. So, every instructor should take due care in fixing the timings of running the centre in consultation with the learners from time to time. If the timings of running the centre are not convenient to the learners, naturally, many of the learners will drop-out and the result will be-failure of adult education programme in that particular centre. The instructors of the present study seem to be aware of this and appear to be running the centre as per the convenience of the adult learners. The observed discrepancy (about 9%) is negligible with reference to this particular role.

Further, with reference to this particular role, the instructors does not feel any difficulty in running the centres as per the convenience of the learners.

When the overall performance of the instructors on this role is taken into account, the following can be said about it. The instructors in general appear to have failed to a large extent in using instructional material like charts, posters etc. effectively to supplement their teaching. By and large the instructors also appear to be less effective in providing relevant information to various occupational groups to improve their skills and in conducting special classes for deserving adult learners to compensate the loss of attendance in the centres. But, the instructors are quite good in using the chalkboard effectively, in stimulating the learners and in imparting literacy skills to the learners. On the whole, when the major role as a whole is taken into account, the instructors appear to be quite successful in discharge of the role.

The low discrepancy (about 19%) observed does not effect heavily.

3. INITIATOR OF DISCUSSION AND AWARENESS

The overall competency of the instructor of adult learners is not measured in terms of his good teaching only. How far he is able to initiate discussion among the learners and how far he makes them aware of various things in and around that matters them. By initiating discussion we mean-choosing a topic of interest to the learners, giving a skeletal frame work to the learners and asking them to fill up the gaps elating to the topic through discussion among the adult learners. The instructor should also guide and correct the discussion as and when necessary. Apart from initiating discussions, the instructor has to make the learners aware of various issues relating to the prosperity and welfare of the learners. Such type of awareness will help the learners to get benefit from various developmental programmes and to be up-to-date in knowledge about the current trends prevailing in the society around them.

The various roles identified to judge the capacity of the instructor as initiator of discussion and awareness according to the present study are as follows:

a) Promote scientific attitude among adult learners.

b) Create awareness about mal-effects of evils like dowry, untouchability, drug addiction, etc.

c) Provide knowledge relating to tenancy laws, minimum wages, developmental schemes, loan facilities and health services.

d) Promote civic sense among adult learners.

e) Awaken the poor and innocent people who are invariably exploited by the vested interest groups.

f) Create enthusiasm among adult learners to learn effectively.

g) Initiate discussion among the learners on varied topics of interests.

h) Encourage the adult learners to share their experiences, skills, and knowledge with co-learners.

In ideal conditions, an instructor is expected or able to discharge all the roles successfully at cent percent level. But, ideology as it is well known always deviates from actual practice of things. It is to be true with reference to the level of performance of different roles by the instructors of the present study in the capacity of as Initiators of discussion and awareness.

The various sub-roles that are identified under the main role 'initiator of discussion and awareness' mean performance of the instructors on each role, level of discrepancy from the ideology and percentage of discrepancy are presented in Table 4.3 in hierarchical manner starting from the high discrepancy mean and ending with the low discrepancy mean.

The instructor during his instruction has to present topics of varied interest to adult learners in a systematic manner keeping in view their mood and interest. Before presenting any topic in such a novel fashion that it creates enthusiasm among the learners to listen carefully what the instructor is going to tell. Such an enthusiasm if he evoked in the learners, naturally draws the attention of learners to listen to the instructor, thus avoiding distractions in between which naturally result in effective learning. The instructors of the sample appear to be quite good in creating enthusiasm among the learners on the topics chosen by them for discussion. The instructors do not pose any problems in creating enthusiasm among adult learners to learn more effectively.

Instruction in the centre will be lively if the instructor gives some introduction to the topic chosen for discussion and then ask the learners to comment and contribute to the topic chosen under his guidance. Such a procedure will make all the learners to be active and attentive towards the programme that is going on in the centre. The learners will have satisfaction of contributing their ideas about the topic discussed at a particular time. This type of procedure indirectly helps to promote co-operative attitude among the adult learners. The instructors of the sample appear to be good in discharging this role as there is only marginal discrepancy (7.24%) in performance of this role successfully. The marginal discrepancy in performing this role by the instructors is attributed to their own limitations in knowledge about various fields.

Whenever discussion on any issue is taken up, the instructor should encourage the learners to share their experiences and knowl-

Table 4.3 : Instructors Mean Performance and Discrepancy Scores and Percentage of Discrepancy for Each Sub-Role of the Major Role 'Initiator of Discussion and Awareness'

S. No.	*S.No. of the Role in Question-naire*	*Description of the Role*	*Mean* Score Points*	*Discre-pancy Points*	*Percentage of Discre-pancy*
1	24	Promote scientific attitude among adult learners.	3.27	0.73	22.32
2	26	Create awareness about mal-effects of evils like dowry, untouchability, drug addiction etc.	3.35	0.65	19.40
3	20	Provide knowledge relating to tenancy laws, minimum wages, developmental schemes, loan facilities and health services.	3.45	0.55	15.94
4	25	Promote civic sense among adult learners.	3.64	0.36	9.89
5	19	Awaken the poor and innocent people who are invariably exploited by the vested interest groups.	6.65	0.35	9.59
6	21	Create enthusiasm among adult learners to learn effectively.	3.78	0.28	7.41
7	23	Initiate discussion among the learners on varied topics of interests.	3.73	0.27	7.24
8	22	Encourage the adult learners to share their experiences skills and knowledge with co-learners.	3.75	0.25	6.67
		Scores on the Major Role as a whole	3.58	0.42	11.73

Note : 240 Adult Education Instructors Represented the Sample of the Study.

* : Maximum Possible Score = 4 Points.

edge if any about the particular issue chosen for discussion with the co-learners. By encouraging the learners for such type of sharing, the instructor will indirectly be providing them a sense of confidence and achievement in the learning activity that is taking place in the centre. The instructors of the study appear to be quite active in this regard and there is only negligible discrepancy of 6.67 per cent in successful performance of this role.

An important aspect the instructor has to keep in mind while promoting discussion and encouraging the sharing of thoughts is promotion of scientific attitude in their thinking and expression. Scientific attitude means, logical reasoning about the good and bad of an issue based on the information available. Such an attitude will help to cut down many biased and prejudiced feelings, ideas and opinion thereby promoting correct version of an issue or thing. The instructors of the sample performed this role only to a satisfactory level as there is notable discrepancy (22.32%) in their successful performance of this role.

The discrepancy in the success of this role is attributed to low response and rigid thinking of the learners for which they are accustomed for a quite number of years. In practice it is really difficult to change a person completely all of a sudden in his way of thinking and reasoning. Slowly and steadily only one can develop this sort of rationalizing the things based on logical judgements.

The instructor is expected to create awareness among the adult learners on evil effects like dowry, untouchability, drug addiction etc. Which are highly prevalent in the present day society. All the learners attending the centres will have some experience or knowledge on the above issues through various media or sources. What the instructor has to do is-choose a topic about which awareness is to be created and discuss the root causes of it, the effects of it on the society at large and the individuals. In particular, ask individual learners to comment on the issue, and then finally add his own comments. By doing so, the learners will be in a position to understand the inns and outs of a problem discussed and develop right attitude about the issue. The instructors of the sample appear to have created awareness fairly well on various mal-effects prevailing in the society. There is notable discrepancy (19.40%) in discharge of this role by the instructors. The discrepancy in discharge of this role according to the instructors is attributed to their own limitations in making final judgements relating to various mal-effects that are prevailing in the society.

One of the important things that should be achieved through adult education is—promotion of civic sense, people should be taught about the rights and duties of a citizen living in a democratic society. Generally, people have the habit of demanding their rights and forgetting their duties as citizens. The instructors should make the learners understand that as citizens while claiming rights, they should also oblige to the responsibilities as members of the society. By proper perspective about rights and duties, the individual will be able to adjust himself in the society and can contribute in his own way for the betterment of the people. The instructors of the sample appear to have promoted civic sense to a fairly appreciable level. The observed discrepancy (9.89%) is attributed to the insufficient supply of material that provides extensive knowledge relating to civic sense to the instructors.

Many of the learners attending the centres, as it is well known, represent the weaker-sections of the community. They may be labourers working for minimum wages, small farmers, or others doing petty occupations and getting meagre income. For such people knowledge relating to tenancy laws, minimum wages and about various developmental schemes which come to their rescue to develop them economically will be of great help. By having knowledge about minimum wages one can avoid exploitation by land lords and the rich. The instructor should make the people aware of the developmental programmes like-Integrated Rural Development Programme, Integrated Child Development Schemes, Training Rural Youth for Self-employment Scheme, Family Welfare Programme, New Twenty-Point Economic Programme, etc. By having knowledge about developmental programmes one can know what type of assistance in the form of loans and subsidies the government is providing to the weaker sections. With this type of knowledge the learner will develop a positive attitude towards learning and activities of the centre. The instructors of the study appear to be performing this duty to a fairly satisfactory level. The instructors feel that insufficient supply of literature is responsible for discrepancy observed (15.94%) in successful discharging of this role.

An instructor is considered to be successful in discharging the major role 'Initiator of Discussion and Awareness' only if he awakens the poor and innocent people who are invariably exploited by he vested interest groups. By vested interest groups we mean people who do things, and who use others as instruments in achieving their selfish desires at the cost of others. Such a type of exploitation will result in vast difference in the class system of society by allowing the rich and powerful become more rich and powerful and the poor deprived of what they should get as their due share for the work done by them. Actually this function is beyond the scope of an ordinary instructor of adults. Yet, what is expected of him is, whole hearted effort in awakening the poor and innocent to the best of his ability without himself being involved in trouble. As per the version given by the instructors of the sample they appear to be performing this role quite well. There is only 9.39 per cent discrepancy in successful functioning of this role.

In general, the following can be said about the performance of the instructors on the above role. The instructors are not very successful in promotion of scientific attitude among adult learners and creation of awareness about mal-effects prevailing in the society. In addition, their success is not highly satisfying with regard to imparting of knowledge relating to tenancy laws, minimum wages, loan facilities, and health services to adult learners. But, in contrast to the above the success rate of the instructors in discharge of the roles relating to promotion of civic sense among adult learners and awakening the poor and innocent people who are invariably exploited by the vested interest group is highly satisfied. Further, the instructors are quite successful in creating enthusiasm among adult learners and encouraging them to share their experiences with co-learners. By and large the instructors of the sample have made a mark as initiators of discussion and awareness among adult learners.

4. ORGANIZER OF CULTURAL AND RECREATIONAL PROGRAMMES

Every individual has to attend to his day-to-day routine based on his occupation and various other roles he has to perform as a member of the society. Doing or attending anything regularly will naturally lead to monotony and boredom to individuals. To get rid of this, cultural and recreational activities will be of great help. By participating or attending in cultural activities, an individual feels freshness and his energies are revitalized to attend to his work with more enthusiasm in the activity. The learning activity of the adult learners can also be promoted by providing them opportunity to attend and participate in certain cultural and recreational programmes. The cultural and recreational programmes can be of various types. Those identified under the major role "organizer of cultural and Recreational Programmes' are as follows.

a) Arrange educative film-shows with the assistance of project Supervisor and other extension agencies.

b) Organise dramas to entertain and enlighten adult learners.

c) Arrange Harikatha and Burrakatha programmes with the help the Project management.

d) Conduct games and sports that are of interest to adult learners.

e) Encourage, Bhajans, Kirthanas that will provide recreation to adult learners.

In ideal conditions, an instructor is expected or able to discharge all the roles successfully at cent percent level. But, ideology as it is well known always deviates from actual practice of things. It is to be true with reference to the level of performance of different roles by the instructors of the present study in their capacity as organizers of cultural and recreational programmes.

The various sub-roles that are identified under the major heading 'Organizer of Cultural and Recreational Programmes', mean performance of the instructors on each role, level of discrepancy from ideology, and percentage of discrepancy are presented in Table 4.4 in hierarchical order starting from high discrepancy mean and ending with low discrepancy mean.

Motion films are often considered as most economic means of recreation for masses in general. But, from the recreational point of view of adult learners, films that give message and information will be of great value. For this purpose, documentary films on various aspects like importance of nutritional foods, family welfare, new twenty-point economic programme, integrated child development schemes, and such other types may be shown to learners. These types of things not only provide recreation but also provide knowledge to adult learners. The instructors of the study appear to be performing this role to a satisfactory level. The wide discrepancy (51.52%) is attributed to lack of facilities to screen such educative films periodi-

Table 4.4 : Instructors Mean Performance and Discrepancy Scores and Percentage of Discrepancy for Each Sub-Role of the Major Role 'Organizer of Cultural and Recreational Programmes'

S. No.	S.No. of the Role in Question-naire	Description of the Role	Mean* Score Points	Discre-pancy Points	Percentage of Discre-pancy
1	30	Arrange educative film shows with the assistance of Project Supervisor and other extension agencies.	2.64	1.36	51.52
2	27	Organize dramas to enlighten and entertain adult learners.	3.27	0.73	22.32
3	31	Arrange Harikatha and Burrakatha Programmes with the help of project administration.	3.44	0.56	16.28
4	29	Conduct games and sports that are of interest to adult learners.	3.58	0.42	11.73
5	28	Encourage, Bhajans, Kirthanas that will provide recreation to adult learners.	3.63	0.37	10.19
		Scores on the Major Role as a whole	3.31	0.69	20.85

Note : 240 Adult Education Instructors Represented the Sample of the Study.

* : Maximum Possible Score = 4 Points.

cally. The instructors emphasize that they cannot do any thing in this matter unless project officers and the field publicity departments co-operate.

Dramas are one of the traditional entertainment forms. To arrange for enacting a drama or to prepare people to participate in drama performance requires lot of preparation and resources. The instructor can motivate the learners to perform simple one act plays which does not require such preparation and resources. The main purpose here should be to promote individual talents in acting and give them an opportunity to participate in them. By this, the learners feel elighted and develop self-confidence on their talents and individual abilities. Further, whenever possible, the instructor can arrange drama shows for the benefit of learners if they can be performed at a low cost. Money for such things, he can raise through contribution by the adult learners. The instructors of the sample appear to be discharging this role to a fairly satisfactory level. Yet, the discrepancy in discharge of this role is significantly large (22.3%).

The instructors feel that arranging drams and motivating the adult learners to participate in drama's needs lot of preparation and time apart from money. They feel that it is practically not possible for any instructor to organise dramas periodically to entertain adult learners. Yet, we notice more than 75 per cent success in discharge of this role by the instructors of the present study.

Harikatha and Burrakatha are traditional type of entertainment particularly for villagers. Through them, lot of knowledge is provided and transmitted to masses on different aspects varying from purana's to Janapada stories. The audience will generally take the message from Harikatha and Burrakatha as the message is passed combining it with lot of humour and practical examples. Arranging them will be comparatively cheaper than dramas. Further, if requested, Harikatha or Burrakatha team may give their programme free of cost for the benefit of adult learners. The instructors of the sample appear to be performing this role quite well as there is about 84 percent success in discharge of this role. The marginal failure in discharge of this role can be attributed to the difficulties in contacting and bringing Harikatha or Burakatha team to some of the villages which are remote and have no transport facility.

One thing the instructor can do without economic problem is, arrangement of sports and games for adult learners. He can conduct and encourage local games like Kabadi running race, jumping, swimming etc. Here also, he can encourage the winners by giving them small rewards. The instructors of the study are quite good in performing this role and as there is 90 percent success in discharging this activity by them.

Every individual will generally be eager to exhibit his talent, if any, possessed by him. Some people will have good and melodious voice for singing. The instructor can encourage such people to participate in Bhajans and Kirthanas to give recreation both for the people participating in them and listening to them. Generally, there is no dearth for this type of activity in villages. This is clearly seen in 90 per cent success of the instructors in discharging this particular role.

On the whole, the instructors of the sample appear to have nearly 80 per cent success in discharge of this major role namely Organizer of cultural and Recreational Programmes. They appear to have organized to the best of their ability Film-shows, Dramas, Harikatha and Burrakathas. Equally well, they seems to have encouraged the adult learners to participate in games, sports, bhajans, and kirthanas. Thus, on the whole, provided a happy cultural and recreational atmosphere for the adult learners.

5. MOBILIZER OF RESOURCES

The success of an Adult Education Programme by an large is determined by the resources placed at its disposal. For a resourceful instructor, generally, there will be no dearth of resources for running the adult education programme successfully. The instructor should carefully look into the physical facilities and the arrangements necessary for the centre taking the assistance of the local people concerned. Further, he should make the best use of the resources in the form of expertise available in and around the centre. Actually, it will be nice on the part of the instructor if he is able to draw a plan of action to involve various types of expertise periodically to enrich the knowledge of the learners attending the centre.

The various roles identified to judge the potentiality of the instructor in mobilizing the resources according to the present study are as follows.

1. Enlist the support of Mahilamandals, Youth clubs, etc., in running the centre.
2. Arrange useful lectures by the experts in various fields to the learners.
3. Use local talents for the promotion of functional skills among adult learners.
4. Procure freely available supplementary reading material like pamphlets, magazines etc. from the developmental agencies and distribute them to the learners.
5. Select suitable accommodation for the centre in consultation with the local leaders and prospective learners.
6. Involve educated youth in running the centre.
7. Enlist community support for the successful implementation of NAEP.

In ideal conditions, an instructor is expected to discharge all the above roles successfully at cent per cent level. But, problems or the obstacles will not permit them to perform the roles to that extent. The various sub-roles that are identified under the major heading 'Mobilizer of Resources', mean performance of the instructors on each role, level of discrepancy from the ideology, and the percentage of discrepancy are presented in Table-4.5 in hierarchical order starting from the high discrepancy mean and ending with the low discrepancy mean.

Proper accommodation is a basic requirement for running of an adult education centre throughout the programme period. So the instructor should be careful in selecting the best place for running the centre within the village limits. For this purpose, he has to take the assistance of local leaders as well as perspective learners. The assistance may be in the form of pursuing some rich men in the village to accommodate a portion of his building or any other structure owned by him for running the centre or it may be in the form of making adjustment of times in the temple place if the centre is to be run in the temple, etc. The instructors of the study appear to have no difficulty in selecting suitable accommodation for the centre. The marginal discrepancy (8.11%) observed is an indication of dissatisfaction expressed by some of the instructors who are not very much satisfied with the accommodation selected for running the Centres in

Table 4.5 : Instructors Mean Performance and Discrepancy Scores and Percentage of Discrepancy for Each Sub-Role of the Major Role 'Mobilizer of Resources'

S. No.	*S.No. of the Role in Questionnaire*	*Description of the Role*	*Mean* Score Points*	*Discrepancy Points*	*Percentage of Discrepancy*
1	38	Enlist the support of Mahilamandals, youth clubs etc. in running centre.	2.63	1.32	49.25
2	34	Arrange useful lectures by the experts in various fields to the learners	3.12	0.88	28.21
3	36	Use local talents for the promotion of functional skills among adult learners.	3.45	0.55	15.94
4	33	Procure freely available supplementary reading material like pamphlets, magazzines etc. from the developmental agencies and distribute them to the learners.	3.70	0.30	8.11
5	32	Select suitable accommodation for the Centre in consultation with the local leaders and prospective learners	3.70	0.30	8.11
6	37	Involve educated youth in running the centre	3.70	0.30	8.11
7	35	Enlist community support for the successful implementation of NAEP	3.80	0.20	5.26
		Scores on the Major Role as a whole	3.45	0.55	15.94

Note : 240 Adult Education Instructors Represented the Sample of the Study.

* : Maximum Possible Score = 4 Points.

their places. The discrepancy refers to non-availability of other better location than their inability in discharging this duty.

The instructor can run the centre successfully in the village only with the co-operation and the support of community at large. Community support may be in the form of encouraging adult learners-to enroll themselves in the Centre, to continue their learning in the centre without break, giving proper hospitality and respect to the outside experts who come to the village to give extension lectures to the learners and so on. The instructors of the study appear to have enlighted the community people very well so as to make them to give their whole hearted support to the programme. This is clear, as the instructors of the sample are able to discharge this function to the extent of 95 per cent success.

Presently, we find sufficient number of educated youth in each village. Many of them may be in search of good jobs or having plans for further education. Generally there will be time gap for these youth either to get into job or for further education after completing a particular course of study. If the instructor can promptly contact these youth, they will definitely do their best for promotion of centre activities as they find no better avocation during the gap period. The instructors of the sample are quite successful in this task as there is only about 8 per cent discrepancy in discharge of this role. The marginal discrepancy in discharge of this role is not due to lapse on the part of the instructor but due to the non-availability of useful educated youth (from the point of view of helping the centre) in certain of the villages.

In many villages especially when they are nearer to the town, we find many organizations for recreational activities found in the towns are also passed on to the villages. The best examples of such organisations are—Mahilamandals, Youth Clubs etc. Generally, we find atleast some people who are active and are interested to do something useful to the public are as members of these organisations. For example, the members of Mahilamandals can run some activities in collaboration with the instructor of the centre or outside agencies. The activities may be in the form of training adult women coming to the centre in skills like tailoring, stitching, weaving, basket-making etc.

Similarly, the youth clubs organize activities like games, sports, organization of dramas, Harikathas, Burrakathas, etc. which will naturally give recreation to the learners in the centre and the villagers at large. There is hardly 50 per cent of success in discharging this role by the instructors of the present study. The large failure in discharge of this role is mainly do to non-existence of Mahilamandals and Youth Clubs in many villages which are remote and not evolved in that extent.

Adult learners attending the centres as it is well known will generally be the people belonging to or performing some vocation or other. So, naturally, their interest in adult education will increase if some arrangements are made in order to promote their functional skills by calling on concerned experts in the field. The experts may enlighten the learners by lectures and demonstrations which are linked to the adults actual work and experience. The instructors of the study are fairly successful (about 84%) in discharge of this role. The discrepancy noted (about 16%) is attributed to the difficulties in utilizing the services of experts in the field in order to promote functional skills of the learners.

The instructors of the adult education centres are by and large people with limited qualifications and knowledge. They can not speak on each and every subject with authority. The experts belonging to various developmental departments like agriculture extension officers and field publicity officers will be of great help in enriching the knowledge of the learners on various issues that are of interest to the learners. All that the instructor has to do is, to contact these experts and arrange lectures to the learners as and when possible. The instructors of the study appear to be discharging this role to a fairly satisfactory level. The discrepancy (about 28%) noted in discharge of this role is largely due to the difficulties in bringing the experts to the villages for utilizing their services.

One way through which the instructor can enrich the knowledge of the learners to the maximum extent with little effort is by procuring and distributing freely available reading material like pamphlets, magazines etc. Some of the pamphlets and magazines are specifically meant for neo-literates and low literate people. This will certainly provide lot of information about various development programmes, modern methods of dealing with various problems, information about various issues etc.

The instructors of the study appear to have sincerely attempted in discharge of this role and as there is only marginal discrepancy of 8 per cent. This too its attributed to lack of sufficient stocks with some of the developmental agencies when the instructors tried to procure them.

The following can be said in brief about the performance of instructors as mobilizers of resources. There is about 50 per cent success in the efforts of the instructors in enlisting the support of Mahilamandals, Youth Clubs, etc. in running the Centre. There is more than 70 per cent success in the efforts of instructors in arranging useful lectures to adult learners. They have made good use of local talents for the promotion of functional skills among learners. The instructors succeeded extremely well in procuring freely available supplementary reading material for learners, in selecting suitable accommodation for the centre and in involving educated youth in centre activities. Further, they have enjoyed excellent community support for the activities of the Centre. On the whole, the instructors enjoyed as much as 84 per cent success in mobilizing the resources.

6. RECORDER OF EDUCATIONAL ACTIVITIES

Apart from instruction the instructor has to keep and maintain a record of various issues relating to teaching learning process for the entire programme period. Record of various activities periodically and their maintenance will be of great help for the instructor as well as for the supervising authorities to review about various issues relating to teaching-learning process and find ways and means of filling the gaps identified during such review. For example, recording the day-to-day progress of the learners in learning will facilitates him to understand at what stage each of the learner stands with reference to the general standard expected of them. Further, maintenance of stock registers, provision of periodical progress reports etc. will enable the project implementation authorities to know the efforts taken by the instructor in distributing learning materials to the learners and his effort in promoting the knowledge of learners. On the whole, the instructor has to play a major role as a recorder of educational activities. The various sub-roles identified to judge the capacity of the instructor in Recording the Educational Activities according to this study are as given below.

1) Record the progress of the adult learners in the three components

of NAEP.

2) Maintain record of the daily events and problems he or she has faced/he or she is facing in running the centre.

3) Provide recorded recognition to the assistance extended by local persons.

4) Maintain a stock register containing details about receipts and issue of materials to adult learners.

5) Maintain the register containing personal information (name, age, sex, occupation and income) of adult learners.

6) Submission of periodical progress reports to the project officer and supervisor.

7) Maintain attendance register and record the attendance of learners regularly.

In ideal conditions, an instructor is expected to discharge all the above roles successfully at cent per cent level. But, practical problems will not permit them to perform the roles at cent per cent level. The various sub-roles that are identified under the major heading 'Recorder of Educational Activities', mean performance of the instructors on each role, level of discrepancy from the ideology, and the percentage of discrepancy are presented in Table 4.6 in hierarchical order starting from the high discrepancy mean and ending with the low discrepancy mean.

The first duty of an instructor as a recorder of educational activities is to maintain attendance register and take the attendance of the adult learners regularly. By doing so the instructor will have an idea about now many learners are attending the centre regularly and how many are irregular in attendance. Once he is able to identify the learners who obtain themselves from the centre for sufficiently longer period, he will be in a position to contact them and find reasons for their absence. If there are any problems that are coming in the way of attending the centre which the instructor can solve or assist, he can do so. The instructors of the sample appear to be quite good in discharging this role as there is about 98 per cent success.

Instead of merely maintaining the attendance of the learners, maintenance of register containing personal information like age, sex, occupation, income etc. of learners will be of further great help in

Table 4.6 : Instructors Mean Performance and Discrepancy Scores and Percentage of Discrepancy for Each Sub-Role of the Major Role 'Recorder of Educational Activities'

S. No.	*S.No. of the Role in Question-naire*	*Description of the Role*	*Mean* Score Points*	*Discre-pancy Points*	*Percentage of Discre-pancy*
1	42	Record the progress of the adult learners in the three components (Literacy, Functionality and Awareness) of NAEP	3.70	0.30	8.11
2	41	Maintain record of the daily events and problems he or she has faced/he or she is facing in running the centre	3.79	0.21	5.54
3	44	Provide recorded recognition to the assistance extended by local persons	3.83	0.17	4.44
4	45	Maintain a stock register containing details about receipts and issues of materials to adult learners	3.88	0.12	3.09
5	39	Maintain the register containing personal information (name, age, sex, occupation and income) of adult learners.	3.90	0.10	2.56
6	40	Submission of periodical progress reports to the project officer and supervisor	3.90	0.10	2.56
7	43	Maintain attendance register and record the attendance of learners regularly	3.91	0.09	2.30
		Scores on the Major Role as a whole	3.84	0.16	4.17

Note : 240 Adult Education Instructors Represented the Sample of the Study.

* : Maximum Possible Score = 4 Points.

solving and understanding the problems of the learners. The problems that hinder the learning activity of the learners may refer to the age factor of the learners, or the sex problems of the learners or the occupation problems of the learners and so on. Background knowledge of these will help the instructor in dealing with the adult learners more efficiently. In discharging this role also the instructors of the sample appear to be quite successful and only very little discrepancy (2.5%) is observed which is negligible.

Once, the instructor takes care about the attendance and personal information of the learners, the next thing he has to do as a recorder of educational activities is, to keep the record of day-to-day progress of the learners in the three components (literacy, functionally and awareness) of NAEP. Such a record will help the instructor to review the progress of the learners periodically as well as to assess the amount of knowledge he has covered during a particular period. Further, such a record will give an idea to project authorities whether the instructor is covering the units he has to cover as per the plan of the programme. The instructors of the sample appear to be performing this activity quite well. The marginal discrepancy (about 8%) observed is attributed to lack of proper measuring instruments to assess the knowledge relating to functionality and awareness of the adult learners.

An instructor, since he has to run the centre in odd hours and has to deal with heterogeneous group of adult learners, naturally faces certain problems sometimes or other in running the centre. Every instructor is expected to maintain a record of difficulties faced by him in running the centre at any time or times. This will help to know and analyse the general problems faced by the instructors in running the centre. The project authorities can think of ways and means of such problems of course keeping their own limitations in view. The instructors of the study appear to be quite alert in recording such events. The observed discrepancy (5.54%) is attributed to the non-serious attitude of some of the instructors to record certain of the difficulties faced by considering them as petty.

It may not be possible for the project authorities to come and check the performance of the instructor or the progress of the learners everyday. In order to make them aware of the progress achieved in the centre, submission of periodical reports is a must. This will make the project authorities to know about the number of working days of the centre, the nature of attendance in the centre, the amount of progress made by the learners in learning activity and so on. The instructors of the study appear to be discharging this function fairly well as there is as much as about 97 per cent success.

Every centre is generally supplied with various types of learning materials and instructional aids. These include slates, slate pencils, janavachakams, roller boards, chalk pieces, charts, maps etc. Apart from these, stock of physical amenities like kerosene lamps are also provided. In order to make the authorities know how these materials are distributed, to whom these materials are distributed, how these are utilized, at what time, etc. details are to be recorded. Such a record will help not only the checking authorities but also the instructor by saving him from the danger of being labelled under misappropriation. The instructors of the sample appear to be quite good in maintaining the stock register and as there is 97 per cent success in discharge of this role.

Recording the activities of the centre and maintenance of the stock register are not sufficient to complete the role of the instructor as recorder of educational activities. He has to keep a separate book where he can enter the details of the persons who have rendered their service for promotion of centre activities and the type of service they have rendered. It will give a sense of satisfaction and pride to such people if you ask them to enter their comments and suggestions about centre activities and take their signature at the end of their comments. The instructors of the study appear to be aware of this fact as there is as much as 95 per cent success in discharge of this role.

On the whole, the instructors of the sample appear to be quite efficient in recording the educational activities of the centre by achieving more than 95 per cent success in discharge of this major role. Their performance on each sub-role is also quite appealing. In recording the progress of adult learners in the three components of NAEP and in maintaining record of daily events and problems faced by them in running the centre, their success rate is more than 90 per cent. In maintenance of stock registers, personal information register and attendance registers, they have achieved more than 95 per cent success. They appear to be quite prompt in submitting periodical progress reports to project authorities. Further, they are quite careful in providing recorded recognition to the assistance extended by local persons.

7. PROFESSIONAL DEVOTION

Present day society is very complex and it requires people with various professional backgrounds and skills to perform various functions in it. Generally, we expect that person possessing a particular professional skill will do his best in his profession. The more a person is devoted to his profession, better will be the results gained. Similarly, in the field of adult education also we require devoted workers who can do their best for the betterment and upliftment of illiterate adult learners. In order to judge the performance of the instructor's professional devotion, various sub-roles can be identified. The sub-roles identified for the purpose of the present study under the major role 'Professional Devotion' are as follows.

1) Enrich personal knowledge by reading books, periodicals, newspapers, etc.
2) Seek advice from experts in adult education in solving problems.
3) Subscribe to an exhibit an understanding of the philosophy of adult education.
4) Assist researches in studies relating to adult education.
5) Use modern methods and techniques in educating adults.
6) Attend staff-meeting convened for adult education instructors.
7) Strive to gain expertise in instructing adult learners.
8) Discuss about better methods of instruction with co-instructors during periodical meetings.
9) Participate in in-service training programmes.

In idealized conditions, an instructor is expected to discharge all the above roles successfully at cent per cent level. But, practical problems or obstacles may not permit them to perform the roles to full extent. The various sub-roles that are identified under the major heading 'Professional Devotion', mean performance of the instructors on each role, level of discrepancy from the ideology and the percentage of discrepancy are presented in Table 4.7 in hierarchical order starting from the high discrepancy mean and ending with low discrepancy mean.

The instructor should be a student constantly and seek new

Table 4.7 : Instructors Mean Performance and Discrepancy Scores and Percentage of Discrepancy for Each Sub-Role of the Major Role 'Professional Devotion'

S. No.	*S.No. of the Role in Questionnaire*	*Description of the Role*	*Mean* Score Points*	*Discrepancy Points*	*Percentage of Discrepancy*
1	54	Enrich personal knowledge by reading books, periodicals, newspapers etc.	3.43	0.57	16.62
2	53	Seek advice from experts in adult education in solving problems	3.61	0.39	10.80
3	50	Subscribe to and exhibit an understanding of the philosophy of adult education	3.74	0.26	6.95
4	47	Assist researchers in studies relating to adult education	3.74	0.26	6.95
5	52	Use modern methods and techniques in educating adults	3.78	0.22	5.82
6	51	Attend staff-meeting convened for adult education instructions	3.80	0.20	5.26
7	48	Strive to gain expertise in instructing adult learners	3.83	0.17	4.44
8	46	Discuss about better methods of instruction with co-instructors during periodical meetings.	3.90	0.10	2.56
9	49	Participate in in-service training programmes	3.92	0.08	2.04
		Scores on the Major Role as a whole	3.75	0.25	6.67

Note : 240 Adult Education Instructors Represented the Sample of the Study.

* : Maximum Possible Score = 4 Points.

knowledge to update himself by reading books, periodicals, newspapers etc. This is very essential because many new things and inventions are coming/every day and unless the instructor is in touch with these developments in some form or other, he will become outdated in no time. By reading newspapers etc. he will be able to understand what is going on around him currently, and will be able to pass on the current information to the adult learners also wherever necessary. The instructors of the study appear to be in touch with certain of the newspapers, books, periodicals etc. to a fairly satisfactory level. A discrepancy of about 17 per cent is noted in successful discharge of this role. The reasons for this discrepancy according to the instructors of the study appear to be non-availability of proper books and periodicals to a satisfactory level to enrich their personal knowledge with special reference to instruction of adult learners.

One of the chief characteristics that help to identify a professionally devoted instructor is, the way in which an instructor behaves in exhibiting an understanding of the philosophy of adult education. By this we mean, the instructor should have a clear understanding of the objectives of adult education, the scope of such objectives, the extent to which such objectives can be realised, the practical problems one has to face in realising the objectives, etc. If the instructor can correctly visualize these things, naturally he will be optimistic in his outlook, tries to make things at ease and will do his best for the realisation of the objectives of adult education. The instructors of the present study appear to be quite optimistic. It indirectly shows their better understanding of the philosophy of adult education. There is only marginal discrepancy of about 7 per cent with reference to this role which can be ignored for all practical purposes. A lapse to this extent is often quite accepted.

The importance of training of adult education instructors not only at the initial stage but also periodically is well recognised by the authorities. In-service training provides the instructors an insight into various issues that are commonly faced by him as well as his co-workers. During the in-service training programmes, he can discuss about such issues with his co-workers as well as with the trainers to find ways and means of solving such problems. Further, in-service training provide the instructor an idea about how the programme is going on in other centres and how his co-workers are tackling the various issues arising from time to time. In addition, in-service training will provide new energy to the instructor in the form of fresh hopes and optimism in running the adult education centre. The instructors of the study appear to be very punctual in attending the in-service training programmes as there is as much as 98 per cent success in discharge of this role.

More than the in-service training programmes, the monthly staff meetings conducted by the project authorities to review the work done by the instructor as well as to know the problems faced by him in running the centre will be of great help for the instructors. In staff meetings, they can freely express and explain about their problems from the point of view of running the centres successfully. The ways of tackling certain of the problems can be known from the combined experience of the instructors. For certain of the problems of possible way of overcoming them can be thought of through discussion. Whenever the instructor finds solutions to the problems he is facing, he gets a shy or relief and encouragement to his work. The instructors of the present study appear to be quite punctual (95%) in attending the staff-meetings.

Successful instruction to adult learners who will be heterogenous in their characteristics will generally be a difficult task. Various ways and means are to be tried out to pass on various types of knowledge to them. Mere lecturing or mere demonstration and so on may not be appropriate to teach all types of information to the adults. To teach about a particular topic, a particular method may be appropriate. During the periodical meetings, the instructor can discuss among themselves the method or methods they have followed to impart a particular unit in the syllabus and the results obtain thereon. Based on their experience, the instructors can decide upon the best method suited for a particular type of lesson unit. For example, to tell about historical event and about a scientific experiment same method may not be useful. The instructors of the study appear to be very alert in this aspect as the success rate is about 97 per cent.

As an extension of their discussion and based on the knowledge gained by them through books, periodicals etc., the instructors can experiment with the new ways and means of passing on information to adults. Such an experiment provides novelty to their teaching and also arouses the interest of the learners to the teaching imparted by the instructor. In fact, many modern techniques of teaching are found to give good results in providing basic skills to even an average intelligent man in an effective way. The instructors of the study appear to be using all the techniques known to them to the best of their ability in teaching the adults.

A good instructor tries to review his instruction every day. Review means—analysing his way of expression, the way he dealt with the adults learners, the way the learners respond to his instruction, etc. In other words, analysis of the interaction that has taken place during he teaching-learning process of a particular day. By such an analysis, a good instructor would like to identify his defects in handling the adult education classes and try to rectify them during the course of instruction. As per the instructors of the study, they are performing this review very carefully and the observed discrepancy is only 4 per cent.

A good instructor should not hesitate to express his limitations and shortcomings to the experts in the field in solving certain of the problems faced by him in successful running of the adult education centre. When the instructor comes out and discusses with the experts freely, solutions to the problems can be found easily. The instructors of the present study appear to be performing this role also quite well. The discrepancy of about 10 per cent observed in successful discharge of this role is attributed to the difficulties in meeting the experts frequently to discuss about the problems faced by them and find ways and means of solving them.

As it is well known, the field of adult education as a discipline is quite young. Lot of research has to be done in order to consolidate and enrich the knowledge relating to adult education. Currently, many educators are interested in doing research relating to various aspects of adult education. A devoted instructor of adults can contribute in his own way to this task by assisting such researchers in their studies. The instructors of the present study appear to be quite generous in this aspect as there is only a meagre discrepancy of about 7 per cent in successful discharge of this role.

Considering the various aspects related to professional devotion of the instructors of the sample, the following conclusions can be drawn. By and large the instructors appear to have good understanding of the philosophy of adult education and have strived hard to realize the objectives of adult education. They appear to have put in lot of effort to enrich their personal knowledge and to gain expertise in instructing adult learners. Their punctuality rate in attending staff meetings and in participating in in-service training programmes is as high as 95 per cent. They have shown keen interest in discussing about better methods of instruction with co-instructors and are quite good in seeking advice from experts in adult education in solving problems. In addition, they have assisted researchers in adult education to a large extent. On the whole, there appears to be about 93 per cent success in discharge of this major role namely 'Professional devotion'.

8. GUIDANCE

In recent times the concept of education has been greatly enlarged and the goals of education have become more comprehensive to include all-round growth and development of personality. Movements in education centered round the needs and purposes of students and demanded that the practices, procedures and programmes of education should be broad based to include physical, intellectual, emotional and social growth. Education should help the people to achieve healthy and effective adjustments to the changing environment. Mere proficiency in the R's is not enough for this purpose. A judicious selection of environmental influences and experiences alongwith wide guidance is necessary to promote allround growth and adjustment.

In a sense, all good teaching involves effective guidance. Effective teaching is gaged by effective learning. Effective learning in reality involves direction and guidance of the learning activities and processes. All learning involves facilitating or strengthening of a tendency of the learners to act to speak or feel in a certain way under certain given conditions. The motives and attitude of the learners determine what activities will provide them satisfaction and consequent learning. The instructor having knowledge of this will come forward with encouragement, help, and guidance so that the learner makes the correct response.

There are various ways in which the instructor can guide the adult learners. Some of the sub-roles identified for the purpose of the present study under the major activity performed by the instructor are as follows.

1) Assist learners of varied interest in procuring reading material to their choice.

2) Assist learners in getting information about various employment opportunities suitable to them.

3) Assist learners in facing academic problems.

4) Assist adult learners in solving their personal and social problems.

5) Identify slow-learners and show special attention to their learning problems.

6) Assist learners in developing study habits.

7) Assist learners in utilizing time profitably.

8) Help adult learners in getting benefit from developmental programmes.

In ideal conditions, an instructor is expected to discharge all the above roles successfully at cent per cent level. But, ideology as it is well known always deviates from actual practice of things. It is to be true with reference to the level of performance of different roles by the instructors of the present study in their capacity of giving guidance to adult learners.

The various sub-roles that are identified under the major heading 'Guidance', mean performance of the instructors on each role, level of discrepancy from the ideology and the percentage of discrepancy are presented in Table 4.8 in hierarchical order starting from the high discrepancy mean and ending with the low discrepancy mean.

Literacy gained by the adult learners will retain long and can be further developed, only, if the adult learners develop proper study habits. By study habits we mean the reading habit, the habit of concentration, the distribution of time for the development of learning skill, etc. Unless the adult learners make reading and writing as a part and parcel of their daily activities, retention of literacy gained by them is difficult. The learners may have problems with reference to reading and understanding from a particular passage. That is, where to punctuate the words, sentences, etc., and understand them in a right perspective. Further, they have the difficulty in concentrating on their study due to diverse distractions. In addition, they may have difficulty in selecting appropriate time for their study. The instructor can come to the rescue of the learners at this stage. He can find out the leisure time of each learner and can suggest them appropriate time for their

Table 4.8 : Instructors Mean Performance and Discrepancy Scores and Percentage of Discrepancy for Each Sub-Role of the Major Role 'Guidance'

S. No.	*S.No. of the Role in Questionnaire*	*Description of the Role*	*Mean* Score Points*	*Discrepancy Points*	*Percentage of Discrepancy*
1	58	Assist learners to varied interest in procuring reading material to their choice.	2.94	1.06	36.05
2	61	Assist learners in getting information about various employment opportunities suitable to them.	3.07	0.93	30.29
3	56	Assist learners in facing academic problems.	3.51	0.49	13.96
4	55	Assist adult learners in solving their personal and social problems.	3.55	0.45	12.68
5	62	Identify slow-learners and show special attention to their learning problems.	3.55	0.45	12.68
6	59	Assist learners in developing study habits.	3.62	0.38	10.50
7	60	Assist learners in utilizing their time profitably	3.66	0.34	9.29
8	57	Help adult learners in getting benefits from developmental programmes.	3.66	0.34	9.29
		Scores on the Major Role as a whole	3.44	0.55	15.99

Note : 240 Adult Education Instructors Represented the Sample of the Study.

* : Maximum Possible Score = 4 Points.

study habit to be continued in a day. The instructors of the present study appear to be performing this role quite well as there is about 90 per cent success in discharge of this role. The observed discrepancy of about 10.5 per cent has to be attributed to the non-cooperative attitude of the adult learners to follow the advice of the instructor.

After devoting to the task of developing the study habits among the adult learners, the next thing of the instructor has to take care of about the adult learners, is their academic problems. Academic problems may be varied in nature. They may refer to reading difficulties, writing difficulties, understanding difficulties and so on. The reading difficulties may refer to word pronunciation, punctuation of sentences, and so on. Writing difficulty may refer to spelling of certain words, writing sentences in an organised way and so. The understanding difficulty may refer to getting the correct idea of facts and figures presented in a lesson unit. The instructor can take proper steps in solving many of the above types of problems faced by the learners. The instructors of the present study appear to be quite helpful to the learners in solving their academic problems. The observed discrepancy of about 14 per cent in discharge of this role is attributed to the uninclined attitude of some of the learners to seek the assistance of the instructor in solving their academic problems.

Some of the adult learners are quite enthusiastic in seeking knowledge by attending the centre. But they may have difficulty to progress in their learning in the same phase with the other co-learners. The instructor has to identify such leaners and show special attention to them by finding practical solutions to cover their slow learning on par with other learners. If the instructor fails to identify and show special attention to the slow learners, however much they may be interested, their interest in learning will not lost long due to frustration. The instructors of the present study appear to be quite good in identifying the slow learners and showing special attention to them. There is about 87 per cent, success in discharge of this role. The observed discrepancy is attributed to the limitations of the instructors in identifying precisely all types of slow learners in the centres.

The adult learners attending the centre will generally be the people with varied interests. Once they get the basic knowledge of reading and writing, they will generally be interest in reading literature that is of interest to them. For example, if the adult learner is a farmer, he will be interested in reading literature relating to better farming. If the learner is an industrial worker, he may be interested in reading literature that gives an idea about the rights and duties that are provided for an industrial worker. Much of the literature of various types described above is freely available through different agencies for the benefit of adult learners. A good instructor should help the adult learners in procuring such useful reading material. But, there is as much as about 36 per cent discrepancy in successful discharge of this role by the instructors of the present study. The above discrepancy is attributed to the passive attitude of the adult learners to strive for procuring such materials.

Adult learners attending the centre will generally the people having settlement in life in some vocation or other. Each adult learner has to perform different roles as a member of the society, as a member of the family, and as a person responsible for his occupation and so on. While discharging so many roles, an individual generally faces many social as well as personal problems referring to his own abilities. Some of the social and personal problems though simple may stand in the way of regular attendance of the adult learners to the centre because of the inability of the learners to find solutions for such problems. The instructor can come to the rescue of the adult learners in such cases and assist them in finding ways and means of solving such problems. The instructors of the present study appear to be quite successful in discharge of this role as there is 87 per cent success. The noted discrepancy of about 13 per cent is attributed to the learners passiveness to take the help of the instructor in solving their personal and social problems.

The adult learners attending the centres may be of varied types. Some of them may be unemployed, and some may have employments of meagre income. Keeping in view, the knowledge about the background information of the adult learners, the instructor can think of suggesting adult learners better employment opportunities that comes across and are suitable for adult learners that come in his way. The instructors of the present study appear to be performing this role to a satisfactory level (about 70%). But, there is as much as 30 per cent discrepancy in performance of this role by the instructors. The instructors consider this discrepancy mainly to the non-availability of such information to them in time so that they can pass on it to the adult learners.

Presently, both the centre and the state governments are showing keen interest for allotting special funds for the benefit of weaker-sections. Many developmental programmes are initiated, and the governmental agencies are at the door of the weaker sections to assist them in all possibilities on application to them. The instructor can assist the adult learners by informing them about such programmes and helping them in getting assistance from such developmental agencies. The instructors of the present study appear to have achieved as much as 90 per cent success in discharge of this role. The observed discrepancy is attributed to the lacuna in getting full information about such agencies by some of the instructors.

Many people in the villages specially, seasonal labourers and women with limited household work appear to be wasting their time in unproductive activities and gossip. The instructor can suggest such people to engage in some economic activity such as toy-making, basket making, netting, etc., which will yield additional income to their family. The instructors of the study appear to be quite successful in discharge of this role also as there is 92 per cent success.

An overview of Guidance role performed by the instructors reveals the following. There is more than 30 percent discrepancy with reference to procurement of reading materials to the choice of adult learners and in providing information relating to employment opportunities suitable to adult learners. But, the success rate of instructors is very high in assisting learners in their academic problems, in solving the personal and social problems of the learners, and in developing study habits among the learners. The special attention shown by the instructors towards slow-learners is also quite appreciable. The instructors have more than 90 per cent success in assisting the learners to utilize their time profitably. Further, the instructors appear to have strived hard to help the learners in getting benefits from developmental programmes.

Sum Up

Taking into consideration the results on the eight major roles identified to be discharged by the adult education instructors, the following can be said about them in brief.

As recorders of educational activities, the instructors of the sample appear to have discharged the role very close to ideology as the success rate is more than 95 per cent. In discharge of the seven sub-roles identified for this role also, in majority of cases the discrepancy from ideology is below 5 per cent (vide Table 4.6). All this go to say that the instructors have kept and maintained a record of various issues relating to teaching-learning process extremely well during the entire programme period.

Professional devotion of instructors of the sample is quite impressive next to recorders of educational activities in closeness to ideal performance. The percentage of discrepancy in performance of this major role which is below 7 per cent indicates the deep commitment of instructors towards their profession. Only in case of two out of nine sub-roles identified under this major role, the discrepancy is above 10 per cent level. In other cases, it is either nearer to the mean discrepancy score or much below it (vide Table 4.7).

In performance of the two major roles namely organizer of the centre and initiator of discussion and awareness, the instructors stand more or less at the same level as the observed discrepancy for these roles is 12.68 per cent and 11.73 per cent respectively. The percentage of deviation from ideology in performance of the majority of sub-roles identified under the major role organizer of the centre is below 15 per cent (vide Table 4.1). This shows that in practice the instructors are working nearly as efficiently as an ideal instructor can organise the centre. In case of majority of sub-roles coming under the major role initiator of discussion and awareness, the instructors are nearer to the ideology more than 90 per cent level (vide Table 4.3). This shows that the instructors are ideally suited to promote awareness among the masses.

The instructors appear to be quite good in discharge of their role as mobilizers of resources with about 84 per cent success rate. The success rate in discharge of this major role would have been much better but for high percentage of discrepancy in discharge of two of the sub-roles identified under it namely, enlist the support of Mahilamandals, youth clubs etc. in running the centre, and arrange useful lectures by the experts in various fields to the learners (vide Table 4.5). Close to the success rate of the above major role is the guidance activity performed by the instructors (84 per cent success). Here also, the gap between ideology and practice would have been much less but for high percentage of discrepancy in two of the sub-roles namely, procurement of reading material of varied interest to the learners and getting information about various employment opportunities suitable to the learners (vide Table 4.8).

The instructors of the sample are about 80 per cent close to ideal instructor in disseminating functional information and imparting literacy to adult learners. The success rate would have been much higher in performance of this role if the observed gaps in discharge of the sub-roles namely, effective use of instructional materials (56.86 per cent), providing relevant information to various occupational groups (39.86 per cent), and taking special classes for deserving adult learners (34.23 per cent) would happened to be at low level.

Lastly, the discrepancy of 20.85 per cent is observed in actual performance of the role of organizer of cultural and recreational programmes by the instructors of the sample. This wide gap (20.85 per cent) would have been much less if the instructors of the sample happened to arrange educative film-shows more effectively (vide Table 4.4).

By and large the instructors of the sample appear to be very successful in discharge of the various major roles assigned to them. They appear to have strived hard to the best of their ability to keep up with the ideology assumed for each of the roles. The gaps observed in performance of various roles can be attributed to the constraints and limitations observed and identified by the instructors with reference to each role. The instructors appear to have tackled equally well all the roles which are diverse in nature. That is, some requiring organising efficiency, some requiring effective teaching skills and some others requiring understanding people and will to serve the needy.

PART—II

ESTIMATION OF SIGNIFICANCE LEVEL OF DISCREPANCY BETWEEN IDEOLOGY AND PRACTICE IN PERFORMANCE OF VARIOUS SUB-GROUP ROLES AND ROLES AS A WHOLE BY THE INSTRUCTORS BASED ON LEVEL OF EDUCATION, CASTE AND SEX FACTORS.

In this part of the study, for each of the chosen sub-group roles of the instructors and for the roles as a whole, analysis of variance was carried out dividing the subjects of the sample based on their level of education, caste and sex. Under the level of education there were two levels namely below 10th class and above 10th class. Under the caste factor, there were two caste groups namely schedule castes (SCs) and Other castes (OCs). Under the factor sex, there were two groups namely men and women. The schematic representation of the subjects of the sample under various groups for the purpose of analysis is as follows.

Variable	No. of Subjects	Total Number
1	2	3
Level of Education (E)		
Below 10th class level	120	240
Above 10th class level	120	
Caste (C)		
Scheduled castes (SCs)	120	240
Other Castes (OCs)	120	
Sex (S)		
Men	120	240
Women	120	
Interaction of Education × Sex (E × S)		
Below 10th class level men	60	240
Below 10th class level women	60	
Above 10th class level men	60	
Above 10th class level women	60	
Interaction of Education × Caste (E × C)		
Below 10th class level SC's	60	240
Above 10th class level SC's	60	
Below 10th class level OC's	60	
Above 10th class level OC's	60	
Interaction of Sex × Caste (S × C)		
SCs Men	60	240
SCs Woemn	60	
OCs Men	60	
OCs Women	60	

Contd.

1	2	3
Interaction of Education × SC × Caste (E×S×C)		
SCs Men below 10th class level	30	240
SCs Men above 10th class level	30	
SCs Women below 10th class level	30	
SCs Women above 10th class level	30	
OCs Men below 10th class level	30	
OCs Men above 10th class level	30	
OCs Women below 10th class level	30	
OCs Women above 10th class level	30	

1. ORGANIZER OF THE CENTRE

As can be seen from Table 4.9 of the three variables chosen namely, Level of Education, Caste and Sex of the Instructors, only Level of Education factor is showing significant F-value (16.16). The

Table 4.9 : Mean Performance Scores of the Instructors of the Sample Grouped under Different Heads and the Calculated F Values for each of the Categories on the Role 'Organizer of the Centre'.

Variable	Mean performance score for the role (Maximum possible score is '4' only)	Calculated F–value
1	2	3
Level of Education (E)		
Below 10th class level	3.455	16.166*
Above 10th class level	3.647	
Caste (C)		
Scheduled castes (SCs)	3.53	0.493
Other Castes (OCs)	3.57	
Sex (S)		
Men	3.52	0.123
Women	3.58	

Contd.

Table 4.9 (Contd.)

1	2	3
Interaction of Education × Sex (E × S)		
Below 10th class level men	3.42	
Below 10th class level women	3.49	1.561
Above 10th class level men	3.625	
Above 10th class level women	3.67	
Interaction of Education × Caste (E × C)		
Below 10th class level SC's	3.43	
Above 10th class level SC's	3.64	0.124
Below 10th class level OC's	3.48	
Above 10th class level OC's	3.65	
Interaction of Sex × Caste (S × C)		
SCs Men	3.49	
SCs Women	3.575	0.085
OCs Men	3.55	
OCs Women	3.585	
Interaction of Education × Sex × Caste (E×S×C)		
SCs Men below 10th class level	3.39	
SCs Men above 10th class level	3.6	
SCs Women below 10th class level	3.47	
SCs Women above 10th class level	3.68	0.219
OCs Men below 10th class level	3.45	
OCs Men above 10th class level	3.65	
OCs Women below 10th class level	3.51	
OCs Women above 10th class level	3.66	

Note : 1) An F–value of 3.84 is significant at .05 level.
2) There were equal number of subjects in all the sub-groups (N = 30 × 2 × 2 × 2 = 240)

F-values of other two variables namely caste and sex are quite low (0.493 and 0.123 respectively) and are no where near the value of 3.84 to be significant at .05 level. Similarly, the F-values for interaction effects between education × sex, education × caste, sex × caste, and education × sex × caste are far below the significant value level. Based on these obtained values, the hypothesis "Subjects of the sample does not deviate significantly from the ideology of 'Organisers of the centres' role assigned in actual discharge due to education, sex or caste differences" is acceptable with reference to the variables caste and sex and has to be rejected with reference to the other variable namely education as its F-value is statistically significant.

The trend can be further examined taking the mean performance scores for the role into consideration. The means show that considerable differences do exist with reference to level of education, caste and sex of the subjects of the sample. Instructors with better education (above 10th class) have better mean performance (3.647) than the instructors with low education qualifications (3.455). There is a difference of .192 in the mean performance scores (which is statistically significant also) which goes to say that higher the education better will be the performance of the instructor with reference to various organisation activities of the adult education centre.

When the instructors are categorized into caste groups, the instructors belonging to scheduled castes appear to be less active than the instructors of other caste groups as there mean scores are 3.53 and 3.57 respectively. Further, when the mean performance scores are considered taking sex into account, women instructors appear to be better in their organising capacity than men instructors as men instructors mean performance score is less by 0.06 points to that of women's mean performance.

The trend of the means in interaction groups reveal the following. Considering the two education groups further dividing them into sex groups also show that education provides superior performance ability to individuals, in general, irrespective of sex as better educated women and men secured better mean performance score than low educated women and men (vide Table 4.9). In addition, women of both educational groups have shown better mean performance scores than men of the two educational groups in comparison to each other.

When the two educational groups are compared considering caste, here also, better educated SCs and OCs secured better mean performance scores in comparison to low educated SCs and OCs. Further, OCs of the both educational groups (above and below 10th class levels) have better mean performance scores than their SC counter parts.

Considering the instructors sex and caste together also, women instructors appear to have better mean performance than men in both SC and OC caste groups. Further, SC and OC women have better mean performance scores than SC and OC men respectively.

On the whole, the following can be said about the trend of results on the role.

1) Instructors with 10th class and above level of education appear to have better organising ability.
2) Instructors belonging to other caste groups appear to be slightly superior to SC instructors.
3) Women appear to be better organisers than men.

2. TEACHER OF LITERACY AND DISSEMINATOR OF FUNCTIONAL INFORMATION

The results in Table 4.10 A indicate that statistically significant differences exist with changes in the level of their education, caste and sex of the instructors in discharging their role as teacher of literacy and disseminator of functional information. Of the three variables, the level of education appear to be highly significant as the F-value is as high as 38.614. It is about ten times more than the value necessary to be significant at .05 level. Caste variable comes next with its F-value of 10.808. The F-value (4.134) obtained for the sex variable though significant at 0.05 level is comparatively small in size with reference to the other two variables namely level of education and caste.

In case of interaction effects, the interaction between education and sex, education and caste are not statistically significant, as there F-values (0.0005 and .549 respectively) are quite low. Similarly, the interaction of education × sex × caste is also not significant statistically due to low F-value (0.61) obtained for it. But, interaction effects between sex and caste show statistically significant differences as the obtained F-value (4.45) is statistically significant at .05 level. The results of the study reject the hypothesis stating that, "subjects of the sample does not deviate significantly from the ideology of 'teachers of literacy and disseminators of functional information' role assigned in actual discharge due to education, sex and caste differences."

The nature of the results can further be examined considering the mean scores obtained for the role. With regard to the level of education, instructors above 10th class appear to be more successful in discharging the role 'teacher of literacy and disseminator of

Table 4.10A : Mean Performance Scores of the Instructors of the Sample Grouped under Different Heads and the Calculated F Values for each of the Categories on the Role 'Teacher of Literacy and Disseminator of Functional Information'.

Variable	Mean performance score for the role (Maximum possible score is '4' only)	Calculated F–value
1	2	3
Level of Education (E)		
Below 10th class level	3.20	38.614*
Above 10th class level	3.505	
Caste (C)		
Scheduled castes (SCs)	3.275	10.808*
Other Castes (OCs)	3.435	
Sex (S)		
Men	3.3075	4.134*
Women	3.405	
Interaction of Education × Sex (E × S)		
Below 10th class level men	3.155	0.00058
Below 10th class level women	3.255	
Above 10th class level men	3.46	
Above 10th class level women	3.555	
Interaction of Education × Caste (E × C)		
Below 10th class level SC's	3.105	0.549
Above 10th class level SC's	3.445	
Below 10th class level OC's	3.305	
Above 10th class level OC's	3.57	
Interaction of Sex × Caste (S × C)		
SCs Men	3.175	4.450*
SCs Women	3.375	
OCs Men	3.44	
OCs Women	3.435	

Contd.

Table 4.10 A (Contd.)

1	2	3
Interaction of Education × Sex × Caste		
SCs Men below 10th class level	3.00	
SCs Men above 10th class level	3.35	
SCs Women below 10th class level	3.21	
SCs Women above 10th class level	3.54	0.061
OCs Men below 10th class level	3.31	
OCs Men above 10th class level	3.57	
OCs Women below 10th class level	3.30	
OCs Women above 10th class level	3.57	

Note : 1) An F–value of 3.84 is significant at .05 level.
2) There were equal number of subjects in all the sub-groups (N = 30 × 2 × 2 × 2 = 240)

functional information' as their mean performance scores are 3.505 and 3.20 respectively. The success rate of the instructors representing schedule caste appear to be slightly less than that of other caste groups as there mean performance score is less by 0.16 points to that of other castes mean performance score. When the means of men and women are considered, women have scored 0.0975 points more than men, thus showing their superiority over men in discharging the role.

An examination of the interaction effect means indicate the following. When the two educational groups are further divided based on sex, women below 10th class level education appear to be better in discharge of the role than men of the same education level. Similarly, women with above 10th class level education proved their superiority over men of the same educational level in discharge of the role as their mean scores happened to be 3.555 and 3.46 respectively.

An examination of the mean performance scores of the two educational groups by further dividing them into SCs and OCs indicate the following. OCs with below 10th class level education can be considered as better teachers of literacy and disseminators of functional information than SCs with the same level of education as the OCs have secured a better performance score of 3.305 in comparison to the mean score (3.105) of SCs. In case of instructors having education above 10th class level also, the OCs appear to be superior to SCs as their mean scores happened to be 3.57 and 3.445 respectively.

When the means are further examined by classifying men and women separately in each caste groups, women appear to be more successful in discharge of the role better than men in case of SCs. But, with regard to OCs, men appeared to be better in discharge of the role than women as their mean score is higher by .005 points. But, this differences is too small and can not be considered as a support evidence to strongly suggest women superiority over men in discharge of the role. Since, statistically significant interaction effects are observed between the sex × caste groups, further examination of the results is necessary.

The results of analysis of variance in Table 4.10 A only indicate that there is significant difference between sex and caste groups. This means, that one or more of the differences among the group means are significant but fails to specify which one of them. Application of Duncan's new multiple range test will illustrate these aspects more accurately which is done as follows.

Teacher of Literacy and Disseminator of Functional Information: Results and Discussion based on Duncan's New Multiple Range Test.

Firstly, significant studentized ranges for 5% level test are noted by looking into the value tables for the sample sizes 2, 3 and 4 (SCW, OCW and OCM). The values obtained for the above sample sizes are 2.772, 2.918, 3.017 respectively. After this, the Shortest Significant Ranges (SSR) are obtained for the respective values of significant studentized ranges by multiplying each of them with standard error. (The standard error calculated and obtained for this particular analysis is 0.4385216). The resulting values are called the shortest significant ranges represented by the symbols (R_2, R_3 and R_4). In the present problem, the values of them are : R_2 = 1.2155, R_3 = 1.2795, R_4 = 1.3230 (vide column 5 of Table 4.10 B).

The differences between pairs of means are tested in the following order : the largest minus the smallest, the largest minus the second smallest, and so on upto the largest minus the second smallest. Then test the difference between the second largest minus the smallest, the second largest minus the second smallest, and so on, until one has tested the second smallest minus the smallest. Because the means are

Table 4.10 B : Teacher of Literacy and Disseminator of Functional Information : Interaction Effects between Sex × Caste based on Duncan's New Multiple Range Test

Groups	SCM 28.5833	SCW 30.4	OCW 30.9167	OCM 30.95	Shortest Significant Ranges (SSR)
	1	2	3	4	5
SCM 28.5833	--	1.8167	0.5167	0.0333	R_2=1.2155
SCW 30.4	--	--	2.3334	0.55	R_3=1.2795
OCW 30.9167	--	--	--	2.3667	R_4=1.3230
	SCM	SCW	OCW	OCM	

Note : 1) Any two means not undersscored by the same line are significantly different.

Any two means underscored by the same line are not significantly different.

2) Explanation of Abbreviations :
SCM – Scheduled Castes Men
SCW – Scheduled Castes Women
OCM – Other Castes Men
OCW – Other Castes Women

ranked in order to magnitude with SCM being the smallest and OCM the largest, the order of testing will involve first finding the differences in column (4) of Table 4.10 B, then those in column (3) and so on moving from right to left.

Each difference between pairs is significant if it exceeds the corresponding shortest significant range. If it does not, then it is not significant. The only exception to this rule is that no difference between the two means can be significant if the two means are both contained in a subset of means that has a non-significant range. Because of the exception noted, it is convenient to group these two means and all of the intervening means by underscoring, as shown at the bottom of Table 4.10 B. No additional tests are made between the means of a subset underscored in the manner described.

Because OCM–SCM is the range of four means, the difference must exceed R_4 = 1.3230, the Shortest Significant Range for four means.

When OCM–SCW value is considered, the observed difference of 0.55 does not exceed R_3=1.2975. Therefore, this difference is not significant and no further tests are made between the means of the subset SCW and OCW. The fact that SCW and OCW do not differ significantly is shown by the underscoring of these two means at the bottom of Table 4.10 B.

In column (3) of the Table, the difference of OCW—SCM = 2.3334, exceeds R_3 = 1.2795 and thus significant difference exists between the means of OCW and SCM. Further the value of SCW—SCM is 1.8167. Since this difference exceeds R_2 = 2155, it is significant. The complete results of the various tests are summarized by the underscoring at the bottom of the Table (vide Table 4.10 B). As indicated under the table note, any two means underscored by the same line do not differ significantly. Any two means not underscored by the same line do differ significantly.

3. INITIATOR OF DISCUSSION AND AWARENESS

Table 4.11 indicates that the performance of the instructors as initiators of discussion and awareness will be better if they have better education background. This is so as there is significant difference (at .05 level) between the performance of instructors with above 10th class level education and that of those below 10th class level education. Dividing and considering the performance of the instructors of the sample under caste groups (SCs and OCs) and sex groups (Men and Women) does not show statistically significant differences even at .05 level due to their low F-values (1.131 and 0.967 respectively).

The F-values obtained due to interaction effects Education × Sex, Education ×-Caste and Sex × Caste does not show any statistically significant differences due to interaction at .05 level. Similarly, the F-value 1.485 obtained as a result of interaction of Education × Sex × Caste also does not show significant interaction effect at .05 level. All this go to suggest that the hypothesis, "Subjects of the sample does not deviate significantly from the ideology 'Initiator of discussion and awareness' role assigned in actual discharge due to Education, sex and caste can be accepted with reference to the variables sex and caste and in case of education variable it is to be rejected.

Table 4.11 : Mean Performance Scores of the Instructors of the Sample Grouped under Different Heads and the Calculated F Values for each of the Categories on the Role 'Initiator of Discussion and Awareness'.

Variable	Mean performance score for the role (Maximum possible score is '4' only)	Calculated F–value
1	2	3
Level of Education (E)		
Below 10th class level	3.502	9.107**
Above 10th class level	3.652	
Caste (C)		
Scheduled castes (SCs)	3.55	1.131
Other Castes (OCs)	3.605	
Sex (S)		
Men	3.545	0.967
Women	3.61	
Interaction of Education × Sex (E × S)		
Below 10th class level men	3.495	2.785
Below 10th class level women	3.51	
Above 10th class level men	3.595	
Above 10th class level women	3.71	
Interaction of Education × Caste (E × C)		
Below 10th class level SC's	3.515	1.742
Above 10th class level SC's	3.585	
Below 10th class level OC's	3.49	
Above 10th class level OC's	3.72	
Interaction of Sex × Caste (S × C)		
SCs Men	3.475	0.048
SCs Women	3.625	
OCs Men	3.62	
OCs Women	3.595	

Contd.

Table 4.11 (Contd.)

1	2	3
Interaction of Education × Sex × Caste		
SCs Men below 10th class level	3.47	
SCs Men above 10th class level	3.48	
SCs Women below 10th class level	3.56	
SCs Women above 10th class level	3.69	1.485
OCs Men below 10th class level	3.52	
OCs Men above 10th class level	3.71	
OCs Women below 10th class level	3.46	
OCs Women above 10th class level	3.73	

Note : 1) An F–value of 3.84 is significant at .05 level.
2) There were equal number of subjects in all the sub-groups (N = 30 × 2 × 2 × 2 = 240)

The nature of the results can further be interpreted based on the mean performance scores of various groups on the role into account. As is the case with the first two sub-group roles, here also, instructors with better education (above 10th class) have better mean performance score (3.652) in discharging their role as initiators of discussion and awareness in comparison to instructors with low education level (below 10th class) whose score is 3.502 only. Instructors belonging to SC group appear to be less successful in initiating discussion and awareness than the instructors belonging to other caste groups as there is .055 points difference between them. When the mean performance of instructors considered based on sex, women appeared to be better than men in the act of initiating discussion and promoting awareness as their mean performance scores are 3.61 and 3.545 respectively.

Instructors possessing below and above 10th class level education when further grouped based on sex, here also, women proved their superiority over men representing similar education group. In each of the two educational groups when the means of SCs and OCs among them are examined, the SC's below 10th class level education appear to be slightly better than the OCs of the same education level in performance of the role. But, in case of instructors with above 10th class level education, the OCs have considerable higher mean score than the SCs which is responsible for providing overall better mean score for the OCs in comparison to SCs. Examination of the mean scores of men and women in each of the caste groups (SCs and OCs) indicate that in case of SCs women have better mean performance score than men. But in case of OCs, men have better mean score than women.

On the whole, the following can be said about the role based on the results.

1) Instructors with better educational qualification appear to be more successful in initiating discussions and promoting awareness among the adult learners (This fact is supported by the statistically significant F-value 9.107 obtained by the duration level groups).

2) Instructors belonging to other castes appear to be comparatively more active than instructors belonging to scheduled caste.

3) Women appear to be better in initiating discussions and promoting awareness among adult learners than men.

4. ORGANISER OF CULTURAL AND RECREATIONAL PROGRAMMES

The results of this role as can be seen from the Table 4.12 are slightly different from that of the other three roles. In case of the other three roles the variable level of education has shown highly statistically significant differences in the nature of performance of the instructors in the respective roles. But, in performance of the role "organizers of cultural and recreational activities", the instructors of the sample does not show statistically significant differences even with reference to the level of education apart from caste and sex variations. This is considered so as the calculated F-values for them (1.364, 2.673 and .0006 respectively) are not statistically significant at .05 level.

In case of interaction effects, the effects are also not significant in case of interaction between education × sex, education × caste, and sex × caste. Further, the F-value of 0.114 obtained due to interaction effects of education × sex × caste is quite low to be significant at .05 level. All this suggest to accept the hypothesis, "Subjects of the sample does not deviate significantly from the ideology of organiser of cultural and recreational programme role assigned in actual discharge of the roles due to Education, sex and caste". With reference to the performance of the instructors on the sub-group role based on their level of education, sex and caste.

Table 4.12 : Mean Performance Scores of the Instructors of the Sample Grouped under Different Heads and the Calculated F Values for each of the Categories on the Role 'Organizer of Cultural and Recreational Programmes'.

Variable	Mean performance score for the role (Maximum possible score is '4' only)	Calculated F–value
1	2	3
Level of Education (E)		
Below 10th class level	3.295	1.364
Above 10th class level	3.3675	
Caste (C)		
Scheduled castes (SCs)	3.385	2.673
Other Castes (OCs)	3.2775	
Sex (S)		
Men	3.315	.00060
Women	3.3475	
Interaction of Education × Sex (E × S)		
Below 10th class level men	3.27	0.114
Below 10th class level women	3.32	
Above 10th class level men	3.36	
Above 10th class level women	3.375	
Interaction of Education × Caste (E × C)		
Below 10th class level SC's	3.30	2.344
Above 10th class level SC's	3.47	
Below 10th class level OC's	3.29	
Above 10th class level OC's	3.265	
Interaction of Sex × Caste (S × C)		
SCs Men	3.375	0.151
SCs Women	3.395	
OCs Men	3.255	
OCs Women	3.30	

Contd.

Table 4.12 (Contd.)

1	2	3
Interaction of Education × Sex × Caste		
SCs Men below 10th class level	3.29	
SCs Men above 10th class level	3.46	
SCs Women below 10th class level	3.31	
SCs Women above 10th class level	3.48	0.114
OCs Men below 10th class level	3.25	
OCs Men above 10th class level	3.26	
OCs Women below 10th class level	3.33	
OCs Women above 10th class level	3.27	

Note : 1) An F–value of 3.84 is significant at .05 level.
2) There were equal number of subjects in all the sub-groups (N = 30 × 2 × 2 × 2 = 240)

A close look at the trend of the mean performance scores of various sub-groups under this role indicate some observable differences. In case of the two educational groups, the trend falls in line in to that of the other three sub-group roles i.e., instructors with higher level of education have proved themselves better in promotion of cultural and recreational activities than the instructors having low education level. In case of caste groups, instructors belonging to SC group appear to be more active in the promotion of cultural and recreational activities than the OC group as their mean performance scores are 3.385 and 3.2775 respectively. When it is a question of distinction of superior performance between men and women, as usual women have proved themselves better than men by 0.325 points improvements in their mean performance score over men.

The following can be said based on the means of interaction groups. When the performance of men and women representing each level of education is considered, in each education group women appear to be better than men in promoting cultural and recreational activities as their mean performance scores are higher to that of men. When the instructors in each of the education group are further grouped based on caste (SCs and OCs), instructors representing SC group in each education level appear to be more active than the OC instructors in the act of promoting cultural and recreational activities. When the mean performance scores of SC men and women and OC men and women are considered SC and OC women instructors appear to be more active than their counterpart men in SC and OC groups. On the whole, though statistically significant differences are not there, the trend of the means indicate that among instructors possessing above 10th class level education women appear to be superior to men. Further, SCs appear to be more active than OCs in promotion of cultural and recreational activities.

5. MOBILIZER OF RESOURCES

Table 4.13 A : Mean Performance Scores of the Instructors of the Sample Grouped under Different Heads and the Calculated F Values for each of the Categories on the Role 'Mobilizer of Resources'.

Variable	Mean performance score for the role (Maximum possible score is '4' only)	Calculated F–value
1	2	3
Level of Education (E)		
Below 10th class level	3.3225	24.375*
Above 10th class level	3.585	
Caste (C)		
Scheduled castes (SCs)	3.465	
Other Castes (OCs)		0.1.60
Sex (S)		
Men	3.3975	4.370*
Women	3.51	
Interaction of Education × Sex (E × S)		
Below 10th class level men	3.28	0.239
Below 10th class level women	3.365	
Above 10th class level men	3.515	
Above 10th class level women	3.655	

Contd.

Table 4.13 A (Contd.)

1	2	3
Interaction of Education × Caste (E × C)		
Below 10th class level SC's	3.355	
Above 10th class level SC's	3.575	
Below 10th class level OC's	3.29	
Above 10th class level OC's	3.595	0.714
Interaction of Sex × Caste (S × C)		
SCs Men	3.425	
SCs Women	3.505	
OCs Men	3.37	
OCs Women	3.515	0.334
Interaction of Education × Sex × Caste		
SCs Men below 10th class level	3.38	
SCs Men above 10th class level	3.47	
SCs Women below 10th class level	3.33	
SCs Women above 10th class level	3.68	4.006*
OCs Men below 10th class level	3.18	
OCs Men above 10th class level	3.56	
OCs Women below 10th class level	3.40	
OCs Women above 10th class level	3.63	

Note : 1) An F–value of 3.84 is significant at .05 level.
2) There were equal number of subjects in all the sub-groups (N = 30 × 2 × 2 × 2 = 240)

Education seems to play a significant role in determining the efficiency of the instructors in mobilization of resources as statistically highly significant F-value (24.375) is obtained for the differences in the level of education. In differentiation of instructors into caste groups (SCs and OCs) has not produced statistically significant results with reference to the fact of mobilizing the resources. But, when the performance of the instructors is considered based on sex, women appear to be better than men as the differences between their mean values are significant at .05 level.

In case of interaction effects, interaction between education × sex, education × caste, and sex × caste have not produced any statistically significant results. But, interaction effects of education × sex × caste have shown statistically significant differences at .05

level. The results of the study partially support the hypothesis, stating that "subjects of the sample does not deviate significantly from the ideology of 'mobilizer of resources' role assigned in actual discharge due to education, sex or caste differences." That is, the hypothesis is rejected with reference to level of education and accepted in case of sex and caste groups.

The trend of the results can further be interpreted taking into account the mean scores of the sample (grouped into various categories) obtained for the role. Instructors with 10th class and above education level appear to be more successful in mobilizing the resources necessary for successful running of the centre than the instructors possessing below 10th class level education (As there mean scores happened to be 3.585 and 3.3225 respectively).

When the caste groups are considered, instructors belonging to SC group appear to have slight edge over the instructors of the OC group, as their mean scores happened to be 3.465 and 3.44 respectively. Women instructors appear to be more active in mobilizing the resources necessary for the centre than men instructors.

An examination of the means relating to interaction effects reveal the following. When the two educational groups are further divided based on sex, women below 10th class level appear to be more successful as mobilizers of resources than men with the same level of education. In case of instructors with above 10th class level education also, women proved their superiority over men in mobilizing the resources for the centre.

The mean performance of the two educational groups on further examination by dividing into SCs and OCs groups reveal the following. Here, in contrast to the general trend, the SC's with below 10th class level education appear to be more successful in mobilizing the resources than OC's of the same educational level. But, when it comes to the question of instructors above 10th class level education, instructors representing of OC group appear to dominate the instructors representing the SC group.

On further examination of mean performance scores of instructors by classifying men and women separately in each caste group, the following can be observed. By and large women in both caste groups (SCs and OCs) appear to dominate the men representing the corresponding caste.

On the whole, the trend of the means indicate statistically significant differences between instructors representing below and above 10th class level education and between men and women. Further, interaction of education × sex × caste has shown statistically significant difference among the means. The results of the analysis of variance of Table 4.13 only show that significant differences exist among education × sex × caste groups. This means that one or more of the differences among the group means are significant but fail to specify which one of them. For further illustration of these aspects more specifically, Duncan's New Multiple Range Test is applied.

Mobilizer of Resources : Results and Discussion based on Duncan's New Multiple Range Test

Firstly, significant studentized ranges for 5% level test are noted by looking into the value tables for the sample sizes, 2, 3, 4, 5, 6, 7 and 8. The values obtained for the above sample sizes are 2.772, 2.918, 3.017, 3.089, 3.146, 3.193 and 3.232 respectively. After this, the Shortest Significant Ranges (SSR) are obtained for the respective values of significant studentized ranges by multiplying each of them with standard error. (The standard error calculated and obtained for this particular analysis is 0.52 9928). The resulting values are called the shortest significant ranges represented by the symbols R_2, R_3 ..... R_8. In the present problem the values of them are : R_2 = 1.4689604, R_3 = 1.5463299, R_4 = 1.598 7927, R_5 = 1.6369475, R_6 = 1.6671534, R_7 = 1.6920601, R_8 = 1.7127272 (Vide column 9 of Table 4.13 B).

The difference between pairs of means are tested in the following order; the largest minus the smallest, the largest minus the second smallest, and so on upto the largest minus the second smallest. Then test the difference between the second largest minus smallest, the second largest minus the second smallest, and so on, until one has tested the second smallest minus the smallest. In Table 4.13 B, the means of the samples are presented in the order of magnitude with BOCM being the smallest and ASCW the largest. So the order of testing will involve first finding the difference in column (8) of Table 4.13 B, then those in column (7), and so on, moving from right to left.

Each difference between pairs is significant if it exceeds the corresponding shortest significant range. If it does not, then it is not significant. The only exception to this rule is that no difference between two means can be significant if the two means are both

Table 4.13 B : Mobilizer of Resources : Interaction Effects among Education × Sex × Caste based on Duncan's New Multiple Range Test

Groups Means	BOCM 22.23	BSCW 23.3	BSCM 23.67	BOCW 23.8	ASCM 24.27	AOCM 24.97	AOCW 25.4	ASCW 25.77	Shortest Significant Ranges
	1	2	3	4	5	6	7	8	9
BOCM 22.23	--	1.07	0.37	0.13	0.47	0.7	0.43	0.37	$R_2 = 1.4689604$
BSCW 23.3	--	--	1.44	0.5	0.6	1.17	1.13	0.8	$R_3 = 1.5463299$
BSCM 23.67	--	--	--	1.57	0.97	1.3	1.6	1.5	$R_4 = 1.5987927$
BOCW 23.8	--	--	--	--	2.04	1.67	1.73	1.97	$R_5 = 1.6369475$
ASCM 24.27	--	--	--	--	--	2.74	2.1	2.1	$R_6 = 1.6671534$
AOCM 24.97	--	--	--	--	--	--	3.17	2.47	$R_7 = 1.6920601$
AOCW 25.4	--	--	--	--	--	--	--	3.54	$R_8 = 1.7127272$
	BOCM	BSCW	BSCM	BOCW	ASCM	AOCM	AOCW	ASCW	

Note : 1) Any two means not undersscored by the same line are significantly different. Any two means underscored by the same line are not significantly different.

2) Explanation of Abbreviations :

BOCM = Below 10th class — Other Castes Men
BOCW = Below 10th class — Other castes Women
BSCW = Below 10th class — Scheduled Castes Women
BSCM = Below 10th class — Scheduled Caste Men
ASCM = Above 10th class — Scheduled Caste Men
ASCW = Above 10th class — Scheduled Caste Women
AOCM = Above 10th class — Other Caste Men
AOCW = Above 10th class — Other Caste Women

contained in a subset of means that has a non-significant range. Because of the exception noted, it is convenient to group these two means and all of the intervening means by underscoring, as shown at the bottom of Table 4.13B. No additional tests are made between the means of subset underscored in the manner described.

Because ASCW — BOCM is the range of eight means, the difference must exceed R_8 = 1.7127272 the shortest significant range for eight means. ASCW — BSCW is the range of seven means, it must exceed R_7 = 1.6920601, the shortest significant range for seven means and so on. When the value of ASCW — AOCM, is taken into account, the difference 0.8 does not exceed R_3 = 1.5463299. Therefore, this difference is not significant and no further tests are made between the means of the subset AOCM, AOCW and ASCW. The fact that AOCM, AOCW and ASCW do not differ significantly is shown by the underscoring of these three group means at the bottom of Table (vide Table 4.13 B).

In column (7) of Table 4.13 B, the difference AOCW — ASCM = 1.13 is a range of three means and does not exceed R_3 = 1.5463299. The underscoring of ASCM, AOCM and AOCW at the bottom of the table shows that these means do not differ significantly. In column (6) we find that AOCM — BOCM = 2.74, the range of six means exceeds R_6 = 1.6369475. However, AOCM — BSCM = 1.3, the range of four means does not exceed R_4 = 1.5987927. No further tests, therefore, are made between the means in the subset BSCM, BOCW, ASCM and AOCM and the fact that they form a subset is shown by the underscoring at the bottom of the Table 4.13B.

The final test obtained is BSCW — BOCM = 1.07 and it is not significant because it does not exceed R_2 = 1.4689604. The complete results of the various tests are summarised by the underscoring at the bottom of the Table 4.13 B. As indicated under note of the table, any two means underscored by the same line do not differ significantly. Any two means not underscored by the same line do differ significantly:

6. RECORDER OF EDUCATIONAL ACTIVITIES

As can be seen from the Table 4.14, in functioning as "Recorders of educational activities", instructors with above 10th class level education have shown better performance than the instructors with below 10th class level education which is statistically significant at

Table 4.14 : Mean Performance Scores of the Instructors of the Sample Grouped under Different Heads and the Calculated F Values for each of the Categories on the Role 'Recorder of Educational Activities'.

Variable	Mean performance score for the role (Maximum possible score is '4' only)	Calculated F–value
1	2	3
Level of Education (E)		
Below 10th class level	3.81	6.839*
Above 10th class level	3.8825	
Caste (C)		
Scheduled castes (SCs)	3.8125	4.897*
Other Castes (OCs)	3.88	
Sex (S)		
Men	3.825	0.366
Women	3.8675	
Interaction of Education × Sex (E × S)		
Below 10th class level men	3.78	0.129
Below 10th class level women	3.84	
Above 10th class level men	3.87	
Above 10th class level women	3.395	
Interaction of Education × Caste (E × C)		
Below 10th class level SC's	3.775	.00001
Above 10th class level SC's	3.85	
Below 10th class level OC's	3.845	
Above 10th class level OC's	3.915	
Interaction of Sex × Caste (S × C)		
SCs Men	3.80	2.214
SCs Women	3.825	
OCs Men	3.85	
OCs Women	3.91	

Contd.

Table 4.14 (Contd.)

1	2	3
Interaction of Education × Sex × Caste		
SCs Men below 10th class level	3.76	
SCs Men above 10th class level	3.84	
SCs Women below 10th class level	3.79	
SCs Women above 10th class level	3.86	0.366
OCs Men below 10th class level	3.80	
OCs Men above 10th class level	3.90	
OCs Women below 10th class level	3.89	
OCs Women above 10th class level	3.93	

Note : 1) An F–value of 3.84 is significant at .05 level.
2) There were equal number of subjects in all the sub-groups (N = 30 × 2 × 2 × 2 = 240)

.05 level. Similarly, instructors representing OC group have shown significantly better performance than the instructors representing SC group in recording educational activities. But, grouping of instructors based on sex has not yielded any statistical significant differences in their functioning with reference to recording of educational activities.

In case of interaction effects, interaction between education × sex, or education × caste, or sex × caste have not yielded any statistically significant differences among the instructors as recorders of educational activities. Similarly, interaction of education × sex × caste has also failed to show statistically significant differences among instructors. Thus, the results of the study indicate that the hypothesis stating "Subjects of the sample does not deviate significantly from the ideology of 'Recorder of educational activities' role assigned in actual discharge of the roles due to education, sex and caste" can be accepted partially only with reference to sex groups.

The nature of the results can further be interpreted based on the mean scores obtained for various sub-groups of instructors on this role. In the case of the two education groups, the trend of the means fall In line as in case of most of the roles i.e., instructors with higher level of education perform their roles better than the instructors with low educational level. In case of caste groups, instructors representing OC's group appear to be superior to instructors representing SC's group as recorders of educational activities as their means scores happened to be 3.88 and 3.8125 respectively. In case of sex groups also, the trend falls in line with the general trend observed for other roles i.e., women proving better than men as the mean scores of women and men happen to be 3.8675 and 3.825 respectively.

An examination of the means of the interaction groups reveals the following.

When the performance of the men and women in each of the educational level groups is considered, women appear to be better than men in the corresponding education level as recorders of the educational activities.

Classification of instructors into SC's and OC's in each of the educational levels (Below 10th class and above 10th class) have shown that OC's proved better than SC's in both educational groups as recorders of educational activities. When the performance of men and women representing SC and OC groups is examined women proved better than men of their caste group in their functioning as recorder of educational activities. ON the whole, the results of the analysis of variance indicate that significant differences exist when the instructors are considered based on their level of education (above 10th class level and below 10th class level) or when grouped based on their caste (SCs and OCs).

7. PROFESSIONAL DEVOTION

Table 4.15 indicates that professional devotion among instructors will be better if they have better educational background. This is so there is significant difference (at .05 level) between the performance of the instructors with above 10th class level education and that of those below 10th class level education. When the performance of the instructors of the sample under caste groups is considered OC instructors performed their role better than SC instructors as there is significant difference between them at .05 level. Dividing and considering the performance of the instructors of the sample under sex groups (male and female) does not show statistically significant differences even at .05 level due to low F-value (1.383).

The F-values obtained due to interaction effects of Education × sex, Education × caste, and sex × caste does not show any statistically significant differences. Similarly, the F-value 3.415 obtained as a result of interaction of Education × sex × caste also does not show

Table 4.15 : Mean Performance Scores of the Instructors of the Sample Grouped under Different Heads and the Calculated F Values for each of the Categories on the Role 'Professional Devotion'.

Variable	Mean performance score for the role (Maximum possible score is '4' only)	Calculated F-value
1	2	3
Level of Education (E)		
Below 10th class level	3.665	12.151*
Above 10th class level	3.8225	
Caste (C)		
Scheduled castes (SCs)	3.6825	6.563*
Other Castes (OCs)	3.8025	
Sex (S)		
Men	3.6975	1.806
Women	3.7875	
Interaction of Education × Sex (E × S)		
Below 10th class level men	3.61	1.383
Below 10th class level women	3.725	
Above 10th class level men	3.795	
Above 10th class level women	3.85	
Interaction of Education × Caste (E × C)		
Below 10th class level SC's	3.61	0.0002
Above 10th class level SC's	3.765	
Below 10th class level OC's	3.725	
Above 10th class level OC's	3.88	
Interaction of Sex × Caste (S × C)		
SCs Men	3.61	0.346
SCs Women	3.755	
OCs Men	3.785	
OCs Women	3.82	

Contd.

Table 4.15 (Contd.)

1	2	3
Interaction of Education × Sex × Caste		
SCs Men below 10th class level	3.50	
SCs Men above 10th class level	3.74	
SCs Women below 10th class level	3.72	
SCs Women above 10th class level	3.79	3.415
OCs Men below 10th class level	3.72	
OCs Men above 10th class level	3.85	
OCs Women below 10th class level	3.73	
OCs Women above 10th class level	3.91	

Note : 1) An F–value of 3.84 is significant at .05 level.
2) There were equal number of subjects in all the sub-groups (N = 30 × 2 × 2 × 2 = 240)

significant interaction effect at .05 level. Thus the hypothesis stating, "Subjects of the sample does not deviate significantly from the ideology of 'professional devoters' role assigned in actual discharge of the roles due to education, sex and caste" can be accepted only with reference to sex groups based on the results.

The nature of the results can further be interpreted based on the mean performance scores of various groups for the role. As is the case with most of the sub-groups roles here also instructors with better education (above 10th class) have better mean performance score (3.8225) in discharging their role as professional devoters in comparison to instructors with low educational level (below 10th class) whose score is 3.502 only. Instructors belonging to SC group appear to have low professional devotion than the instructors belonging to other castes as there is 0.12 points difference between them. When the mean performance scores of instructors is considered based on sex, women appear to have better professional devotion than men as their mean scores are 3.7875 and 3.6825 respectively.

Instructors possessing below and above 10th class level education when further grouped based on sex, here also women proved their superiority over men representing similar education group. When we examine the mean scores of men and women in each of the caste groups (SCs and OCs) women have better mean performance scores than men in both the caste groups.

On the whole, the following can be said about the role based on the results.

1. Instructors with better educational qualification appear to show more professional devotion (This is supported by the statistically significant F-value 12.151 obtained for the educational level groups).

2. Instructors belonging to other castes show more professional devotion than instructors belonging to scheduled castes.

3. Women appear to have more professional devotion than men.

8. GUIDANCE

As can be seen from Table 4.16, Education seems to play a significant role in determining the capacity of the instructors in 'Guidance' activities as statistically significant F-value (14.916) is obtained for the differences in the levels of education. Differentiation of instructors into caste groups (SCs and OCs) and sex groups (men and women) have not produced statistically significant results (F-values 1.385 and 0.347 respectively) with reference to the activity of giving guidance to adult learners.

In case of interaction effects, interaction between education × sex, or education × caste, or sex × caste have not yielded any statistically significant differences among instructors in doing guidance activity. Similarly, interaction of education × sex × caste has also failed to show statistically significant differences among instructors representing this group. So, the hypothesis, stating that "subjects of the sample does not deviate significantly from the ideology of 'Guidance' role assigned in actual discharge due to education, sex or caste" is partially rejected only with reference to level of education.

The trend of the results can be further interpreted taking into account the mean scores of the sample (grouped into various categories) obtained for the role. With regard to the level of education, instructors with above 10th class qualification appear to be more successful in giving guidance to adult learners than instructors with below 10th class qualification as their mean performance scores are 3.555 and 3.3375 respectively. The success rate of the instructors representing other castes appear to be slightly better than that of the scheduled caste groups as the mean performance score of OCs is

Table 4.16 : Mean Performance Scores of the Instructors of the Sample Grouped under Different Heads and the Calculated F Values for each of the Categories on the Role 'Guidance' (to adult learners).

Variable	Mean performance score for the role (Maximum possible score is '4' only)	Calculated F–value
1	2	3
Level of Education (E)		
Below 10th class level	3.3375	14.916*
Above 10th class level	3.555	
Caste (C)		
Scheduled castes (SCs)	3.4125	1.385
Other Castes (OCs)	3.48	
Sex (S)		
Men	3.3675	0.347
Women	3.525	
Interaction of Education × Sex (E × S)		
Below 10th class level men	3.25	3.658
Below 10th class level women	3.425	
Above 10th class level men	3.485	
Above 10th class level women	3.625	
Interaction of Education × Caste (E × C)		
Below 10th class level SC's	3.325	0.541
Above 10th class level SC's	3.5	
Below 10th class level OC's	3.35	
Above 10th class level OC's	3.61	
Interaction of Sex × Caste (S × C)		
SCs Men	3.325	3.519
SCs Women	3.5	
OCs Men	3.41	
OCs Women	3.55	

Contd.

Table 4.16 (Contd.)

1	2	3
Interaction of Education × Sex × Caste		
SCs Men below 10th class level	3.20	
SCs Men above 10th class level	3.45	
SCs Women below 10th class level	3.45	
SCs Women above 10th class level	3.55	
OCs Men below 10th class level	3.30	1.299
OCs Men above 10th class level	3.52	
OCs Women below 10th class level	3.40	
OCs Women above 10th class level	3.70	

Note : 1) An F–value of 3.84 is significant at .05 level.
2) There were equal number of subjects in all the sub-groups (N = 30 × 2 × 2 × 2 = 240)

0.0675 points more than that of SCs. When the means of men and women are considered, women have scored 0.1575 points more than men, thus showing their superiority over men in discharging the role.

An examination of the interaction effects means indicate the following. When the educational groups are further divided based on sex, women below 10th class level education appear to be better in discharge of the role than men of the same educational level. Similarly, women with above 10th class level education proved their superiority over men of the same educational level in discharge of the role as their mean performance scores happened to be 3.625 and 3.485 respectively.

An examination of the mean performance scores of the two educational groups by further dividing them into SCs and OCs indicate the following. OCs with below and above 10th class level education can be considered better than SCs with same educational level in giving guidance to adult learners.

Further, examination of the mean performance scores of instructors by classifying men and women separately in each caste group, the following can be observed. By and large women in both caste groups (SCs and OCs) appear to be better guides than men representing the corresponding caste groups.

On the whole, the following can be said about the trend of the results on the role.

1. Instructors with 10th class and above level of education appear to be more successful in giving guidance to adult learners.
2. Instructors belonging to other caste groups appear to be slightly superior to SC instructors in guiding adult learners.
3. Women instructors appear to be better in guiding the adult learners than men instructors.

9. ESTIMATION OF SIGNIFICANCE LEVEL OF DISCREPANCY BETWEEN IDEOLOGY AND PRACTICE IN DISCHARGE OF VARIOUS ROLES (AS A WHOLE) BY THE INSTRUCTORS BASED ON LEVEL OF EDUCATION, CASTE AND SEX FACTORS

After looking into the discrepancy between ideology and practice in performance of various sub-groups roles, discrepancy estimation was done for overall performance of the roles by the instructors, considering the same factors namely : Education, Caste and Sex. The details of the results are as follows.

Table 4.17 indicates that the overall performance of the instructor on various roles assigned to them will be better if they have better education background. This is so as there is significant difference (F-value 39.174) at .05 level between the performance of instructors with above 10th class level education and below 10th class level education. The F-values of other two variables namely caste and sex are not showing statistically significant differences (F-values 3.632 and 0.721 respectively) at .05 level. But, the F-value of the variable namely caste (3.632) is nearer to the value of 3.84 to be significant at 0.05 level. Similarly, the F-values for interaction effects between Education × sex; Education × caste; Sex × caste; and Education × sex × caste are far below the significant value level. Based on this obtained values the hypothesis, "Subjects of the sample does not deviate significantly from the ideology of roles assigned to them in actual discharge due to education, sex and caste" is acceptable with reference to the variables sex and caste and has to be rejected with reference to the other variable namely education.

The trend can be further examined taking the mean performance scores into consideration. In case of the two education groups,

Table 4.17 : Mean Performance Scores of the Instructors of the Sample Grouped under Different Heads and the Calculated F Values for each of the Categories.

Variable	Mean performance score for the role (Maximum possible score is '4' only)	Calculated F–value
1	2	3
Level of Education (E)		
Below 10th class level	3.449375	39.174*
Above 10th class level	3.6275	
Caste (C)		
Scheduled castes (SCs)	3.5153125	3.632
Other Castes (OCs)	3.5615625	
Sex (S)		
Men	3.49787125	0.721
Women	3.5790625	
Interaction of Education × Sex (E × S)		
Below 10th class level men	3.4075	1.860
Below 10th class level women	3.49125	
Above 10th class level men	3.588125	
Above 10th class level women	3.66875	
Interaction of Education × Caste (E × C)		
Below 10th class level SC's	3.426875	0.033
Above 10th class level SC's	3.60375	
Below 10th class level OC's	3.471875	
Above 10th class level OC's	3.65125	
Interaction of Sex × Caste (S × C)		
SCs Men	3.46125	0.00006
SCs Women	3.569375	
OCs Men	3.534375	
OCs Women	3.58875	

Contd.

Table 4.17 (Contd.)

1	2	3
Interaction of Education × Sex × Caste		
SCs Men below 10th class level	3.37375	
SCs Men above 10th class level	3.54875	
SCs Women below 10th class level	3.48	
SCs Women above 10th class level	3.65875	2.248
OCs Men below 10th class level	3.44125	
OCs Men above 10th class level	3.6275	
OCs Women below 10th class level	3.5025	
OCs Women above 10th class level	3.675	

Note : 1) An F–value of 3.84 is significant at .05 level.
2) There were equal number of subjects in all the sub-groups (N = 30 × 2 × 2 × 2 = 240)

instructors with higher level of education proved themselves better in performing their roles than the instructors who are having low educational level as their mean performance scores are 3.6275 and 3.4493 respectively. In case of caste groups, instructors belonging to OC group appear to be more active in discharging their roles effectively than the SC group as their mean performance scores are 3.5615 and 3.5153 respectively. When the performance scores of men and women are considered woman have proved their superiority over men by scoring .08125 points more than men.

The following can be said based on the means of interaction groups. When the performance of men and women representing each level of education is considered, women appear to be better than men in discharging their roles as their mean performance scores are higher to that of men. When instructors in each of the education group are further grouped based on caste (SC's and OC's), instructors representing OC group in each education level appear to be more successful than the SC instructors. The mean performance scores of SC men and women and OC men and women show that SC and OC women instructors appear to be more successful than their counterpart men in SC and OC groups. Further, OC men and women are more active than SC men and women in discharging their roles.

On the whole, the following can be said about the overall role performance of the instructors.

1) Instructors with better educational qualification appear to be more successful in discharging their roles. (This fact is supported by the statistically significant F-value 39.174 obtained by the education level groups).

2) Instructors belonging to other castes appear to be comparatively more active than instructors belonging to scheduled castes in successful discharge of their roles.

3) Women instructors appear to be more successful in discharging their roles than men instructors.

5
Summary and Conclusion

INTRODUCTION

The instructor of adults is expected to play many roles. He has instructional responsibilities, counselling responsibilities, professional growth responsibilities, curriculum development responsibilities, public relations responsibilities and others as well. In recent years the instructional role of the instructor has changed from a disseminator of information to that of an instructional manager. As an instructional manager, the instructor is responsible for creating an environment where learning can take place. In this role, instructor determines learning objectives, diagnose learners, plan learning activities, implement programmes and evaluates learners progress.

The various roles expected of instructor of adults are : organizer of the centre; teacher of literacy and disseminator of functional information; initiator of discussion and awareness; organiser of cultural and recreational programmes; mobilizer of resources; recorder of educational activities; devotion to profession; and effective guidance to adult learners.

The diversity of roles listed above appear to be quite ambitious when considered in terms of the qualifications and honorarium paid to the instructors. In order to be successful in performing his roles, the instructor has to shoulder many responsibilities, adopt to many situations, and exercise leadership under multitude of circumstances.

This means, instructors should have strong will and at the same time adoptability to a variety of conditions. The adult education instructors with their background may find it difficult to perform the various roles expected of them in an ideal way. Gaps are certain to exist between the achieved and expected role performance of the instructors.

OBJECTIVES OF THE STUDY

Based on the above illustration, the objectives of the study were:

1) to estimate the amount of discrepancy that exist between idealized performance of each role assigned to the instructor and that discharged in actual practice;
2) to know the reasons that cause discrepancy in successful discharge of each role assigned to the instructor; and
3) to study the amount of discrepancy that exists in actual performance of roles from the ideology due to education, sex and caste differences.

HYPOTHESES

Based on the problem the following hypotheses were framed for testing.

MAJOR HYPOTHESES

The subjects of the sample does not deviate significantly from the ideology of various roles assigned to them in actual discharge due to education, sex or caste differences.

In the light of the major hypothesis, the following sub-hypotheses were framed.

1) Subjects of the sample does not deviate significantly from the ideology of 'organizers of the centres' role assigned in actual discharge due to education, sex or caste differences.
2) Subjects of the sample does not deviate significantly from the ideology of 'teachers of literacy and disseminators of functional information', role assigned in actual discharge due to education, sex or caste differences.
3) Subjects of the sample does not deviate significantly from

the ideology of 'initiators of discussion and awareness' role assigned in actual discharge due to education, sex or caste differences.

4) Subjects of the sample does not deviate significantly from the ideology of 'organisers of cultural and recreational programmes' role assigned in actual discharge due to education, sex, or caste differences.

5) Subjects of he sample does not deviate significantly from the ideology of 'mobilizers of resources' role assigned in actual discharge due to education, sex or caste differences.

6) Subjects of the sample does not deviate significantly from the ideology of 'recorders of educational activities' role assigned in actual discharge due to education, sex or caste differences.

7) Subjects of the sample does not deviate significantly from the ideology of 'devotors to profession' role assigned in actual discharge due to education, sex or caste differences.

8) Subjects of the sample does not deviate significantly from the ideology of 'guidance' role assigned in actual discharge due to education, sex or caste differences.

SUBJECTS OF STUDY

For the purpose of the present investigation, National Adult Education Programme (NAEP) instructors (who have completed or about to complete their term as instructors) representing caste groups, sex groups, and education groups were required. On the whole, for the purpose of the present study a sample of 240 instructors representing caste, sex, and education groups were randomly chosen from the lists of instructors working in Sri Kalahasti and Naidupet Projects, Chittoor District, Andhra Pradesh.

The details of the sample graphically represented on page 115.

METHOD OF STUDY

A questionnaire was constructed covering the 8 major roles expected of instructors.

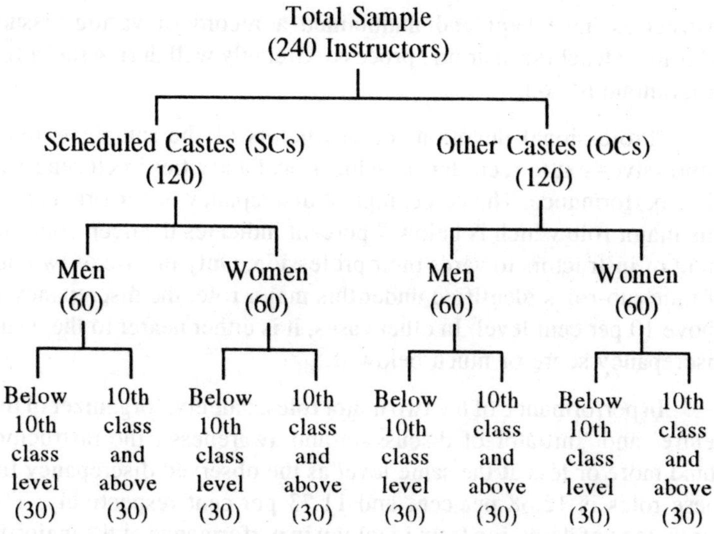

The answers given by instructors for questions under each role were tabulated taking the scores given in gradation against each question/statement. The discrepancy for each role was calculated in terms of percentages. To know the discrepancy in discharge of each major role and roles as a whole with reference to education, sex and caste, the analysis of variance was carried out. Wherever the F-values were significant, to know further significance within each education, sex or caste group, the Duncan's test was carried out.

FINDINGS OF THE STUDY

Part I

The findings of the study are discussed in two parts. In Part I, the discrepancy that exists in actual performance of the roles by the instructors in comparison to the idealized performance of the roles is discussed in terms of percentages. The details of it in brief are as follows.

As 'recorders of educational activities', the instructors of the sample appear to have discharged the role very close to ideology as the success rate is more than 95 per cent. In discharge of the seven sub-roles identified for this role also, in majority of cases the discrepancy from ideology is below 5 per cent. All this go to say that the instructors have kept and maintained a record of various issues relating to teaching-learning process extremely well during the entire programme period.

'Professional devotion' of instructors of the sample is quite impressive next to recorders of educational activities in closeness to ideal performance. The percentage of discrepancy in performance of this major role which is below 7 percent indicates the deep commitment of instructors towards their profession. Only in case of two out of nine sub-roles identified under this major role, the discrepancy is above 10 per cent level. In other cases, it is either nearer to the mean discrepancy score or much below it.

In performance of the two major roles, namely, 'organizer of the centre' and 'initiator of discussion and awareness', the instructors stand more or less at the same level as the observed discrepancy for these roles is 12.68 per cent and 11.73 per cent respectively. The percentage of deviation from ideology in performance of the majority of sub-roles identified under the major role organizer of the centre is below 15 per cent. This shows that in practice the instructors are working nearly as efficiently as an ideal instructor can organize the centre. In case of majority of sub-roles coming under the major role initiator of discussion and awareness the instructors are nearer to the ideology at more than 90 per cent level. This shows that the instructors are ideally suited to promote awareness among the masses.

The instructors appear to be quite good in discharge of their role 'mobilizers of resources' with about 84 per cent success rate. The success rate in discharge of this major role would have been much better but for high percentage of discrepancy in discharge of two of the sub-roles identified under it namely, 'enlist the support of Mahilamandals, youth clubs etc. in running the centre', and 'arrange useful lectures by the experts in various fields to the learners'. Close to the success rate of the above major role is the guidance activity performed by the instructors (84% success). Here also, the gap between ideology and practice would have been much less but for high percentage of discrepancy in two of the sub-roles namely, procurement of reading material of varied interest to the learners and, getting information about various employment opportunities suitable to the learners.

The instructors of the sample are about 80 per cent close to ideal instructor in disseminating functional information and imparting literacy to adult learners. The success rate would have been much higher in performance of this role if the observed gaps in discharge of the sub-roles namely, effective use of instructional materials (56.86%), providing relevant information to various occupational groups (39.86%) and taking special classes for deserving adult learners (34.23%) would happened to be at low level.

Lastly, the discrepancy of 20.85 per cent is observed in actual performance of the role 'organizer of cultural and recreational programmes' by the instructors of the sample. This wide gap (20.85 per cent) would have been much less if the instructors of the sample happened to arrange educative film-shows more effectively.

By and large and instructors of the sample appear to be very successful in discharge of the various major roles assigned to them. They appear to have strived hard to the best of their ability to keep up with the ideology assumed for each of roles. The gaps observed in performance of various roles can be attributed to the constraints and limitations observed and identified by the instructors with reference to each role. The instructors appear to have tackled equally well all the roles which are diverse in nature. That is, some requiring organizing efficiency, some requiring effective teaching skills and, some others requiring understanding people and will to serve the needy.

Part II

In Part II of the study, the role performance of the instructors with reference to education, sex and caste is discussed for all the 8 sub-roles identified for the study as well as for the roles as a whole. The summary of discussion on the above is as follows.

In case of the role 'organizer of the centre' the trend of the results indicate the following : (1) Instructors with 10th class and above level of education appear to have better organising ability, (2) Instructors belonging to other caste groups appear to be slightly superior to scheduled castes (SCs) instructors, (3) Women appear to be better organisers than men.

With reference to the role 'teacher of literacy and disseminator of functional information' indicated that better performance goes with better education. Women appear to be better than men in performance of the role. further, instructors of other caste seems to be better teachers of literacy and disseminators of functional information.

The results on the role 'initiator of discussion and awareness' indicate the following.

(1) Instructors with better educational qualification appear to be more successful in initiating discussions and promoting awareness among the adult learners, (2) Instructors belonging to other castes appear to be comparatively more active than instructors belonging to scheduled castes, (3) Women appear to be better in initiating discussions and promoting awareness among adult learners than men.

No significance differences were found in performance of the role 'organizer of cultural and recreational programmes' with reference to level of education, caste and sex.

The results on the role 'mobilizers of resources' indicates that higher the education better will be resource mobilization ability for instructors. Further, women seems to be better mobilizers of resources than men.

The results on the roles 'recorder of educational activities' and 'professional devotion' show that higher the level of education better will be the performance on these roles. Further, SC instructors seem to be slightly less efficient than other caste group instructors in performance of these roles.

Lastly performance of 'Guidance' role reveal the following : (1) Instructors with 10th class and above level of education appear to be more successful in giving guidance to adult learners, (2) Instructors belonging to other caste groups appear to be slightly superior to SC instructors in guiding adult learners, (3) Women instructors appear to be better in guiding the adult learners than men instructors.

On the whole, the following can be said about the role performance of the instructors.

(1) Instructors with better educational qualification appear to be more successful in discharging their roles, (2) Instructors belonging to other castes appear to be comparatively more active than instructors belonging to scheduled castes, in successful discharge of their roles. (3) Women instructors appear to be more successful in discharging their roles than men instructors.

SUGGESTIONS FOR FURTHER RESEARCH

Firstly, similar study can be undertaken on a fairly large number of sample. Secondly, in the present study discrepancy is noted based on the instructors rating only. The study can be made more assertive by taking the ratings from learners (who have completed the course under the instructors) as well as from the community leaders. Thirdly, studies illustrating the effect of social psychological factors on the role-performance of the instructors can be undertaken. The scope for studies on adult education instructors is vast. Indepth studies can be undertaken to know the effect of factors like attitude of instructors, motivation of instructors etc. on role success.

Bibliography

Adaval, S.B. (1952). *An investigation into the qualities of teachers under training*. Unpublished Ph.D. Thesis, Allahabad University.

Aker, G.F. (1962). *The identification of criteria for evaluating graduate programmes in adult education*. Unpublished Doctoral dissertation; University of Winsconsin.

Armstrong, D.G., Henson, K.T., Savage, T.V. (1981). *Education : An Introduction*. New York : Macmillan Publishing. Inc.

Aphrodite, B. (1981). *Continuing Education needs of Adult Educators*. Doctoral dissertation; University of Missouri-Columbia.

Barr, A.S. and Others. (1935). Validity of certain instruments employed in the measurement of teaching ability. *Measurement of Teaching Efficiency*, New York : Macmillan.

Beamer, G.C. and Ledbetter, EW. (1957). The Relation between teacher attitude and the social service interest. *Journal of Educational Research*. 50, pp. 655–666.

Bledsoe, J.C. and Brown, D. (1968). Role perceptions of Secondary Teachers as related to pupils perceptions of teacher behavioural characteristics. *The Journal of Educational Research*, Vol. 61, No. 9, pp. 422–429.

Biddle, B.J. and Edqin J. Thomas, eds. (1966). *Role Theory—Concepts and Research*. New York, Wiley.

Bhatia, B.D. and Bhatia, K. (1981). *The principles and methods of teaching*. Doaba House, Delhi—6.

Buch, M.B. (Ed) (1974). *A Study of Research in Education*, CASE, M.S. University of Baroda, Baroda.

Chamberlain, M.M. (1960). The competencies of Adult Educators. *Adult Education*, 11, pp.. 81–82.

Chhaya, (1974). *An Investigation into certain psychological characteristics of an effective school teacher (A comparative study of effective and ineffective teachers)*. Ph.D. Thesis, Kanpur University.

Cattell, R.B. (1950). *Personality : A systematic, Theoretical and Factual Study*. New York : McGraw Hill Book Company, pp. 2–3.

Debnath, N.N. (1971). *Teaching efficiency, its measurement and some determinants*. Ph.D. Thesis, Viswabharathi University.

Deva, R.C. (1966). *Prediction of Student Teaching Success*. Dissertation, Aligarh Muslim University.

Directorate of Adult Education : Ministry of Education and Social Welfare; *Training of Adult Education Functionaries, A Hand-Book*, Government of India, New Delhi.

Fox, W.H. and Richey (1948). An analysis of various fctors associated with selection of teaching as a vocation. Indian University School of Bulletin, 24, pp. 1–58.

Freehill, M.F. (1963). A prediction of the teaching competence. *Journal of Experimental Education*, 31, pp. 307–311.

Freeman, F.S. (1962). *Theory and practical of psychological testing*. Oxford and Publishing Company, New Delhi.

Gage, N.L. (1965). *Desirable behaviours of teachers*. Urban Education, 1: pp. 85–95.

Ganeless, D. (1974). Competency — Based preparation programmes for teachers of Adults. *Adult Leadership*, 23, p. 188.

Grabowski, S.M. (1976). *Training teachers of adults : Modes and Innovative Programmes*. Washington, D.C : National Institute of Education (ERIC, Document Reproduction Service No. ED

131, 184).

Gupta, A.K. (1984). *Teacher Education, Current and Prospects.* Sterling Publishers Pvt. Ltd., L-10, Green Park Extension , New Delhi — 110 016.

Gupta, R.C. (1975). *Prediction of Teacher Effectiveness through personality test.* Ph.D. Thesis, B.H.U.

Gupta, R.N. (1977). A Study of the Personality Traits of Primary School Teachers. *Journal of Educational Research and Extension,* Vol. 14, No. 1.

Gupta, V.P. (1977). *Personality Characteristics, Adjustment Level, Academic Achievement and Professional Attitude of Successful Teachers.* Ph.D. Thesis, Punjab University.

Goyal, R.P. (1974). *A Study of Some of the Personality correlates of creativity in Secondary School teachers under training.* Ph.D. Thesis, Punjabi University.

Gross, N., Mason, W.S., and McEachern, W.B. (1958) *Explorations in Role Analysis : Studies in the School Superintendency Role,* New York; Wiley.

Hampton, N.D. (1951) An analysis of Supervisory ratings of elementary teachers graduate from Iowa State Teachers College. *Journal of Experimental Education,* 20, pp. 179–216.

International Institute for Literacy Methods. (1978). *Literacy Teachers : Interpretive Bibliography.* Printed and published by International Institute for Adult Literacy Methods : P.O. Box. 1555, Tehran, Iran.

Jain, J.C. and Kapoor, H.K. (1980). *Refresher Course in Modern Indian Education and Its Problems.* Published by Ramparkash Tandon, Prakash Brothers, Books Market, Ludhiana.

Jasper, J. Valenti and Charles W. Nelson, W. (1951). Survey Teaching Practices (Chicago; Science Research Associates, 1951).

Kaul, L (1972). Personality differentia of Popular Teachers. *Journal of Educational Psychology,* Vol. XXXI, No. 2, Sardar Patel University, Vallabh Vidyanagar, Gujarat.

Lamake, A.T. (1951). Personality and Teaching Success. *Journal of*

Experimental Education, Vol. : 20, No. 2. pp. 217–259.

Leeds, C.H (1956). Teacher attitude and temperament as a measure of teacher-pupil rapport. *Journal of Applied Psychology*, 40, pp. 333–337.

Lindgreen, H.C. and Pattan, C.M. (1958). Attitude of High School and other teachers twards children and current educational methodology, California. *Journal of Educational Research*, pp. 80–85.

Macomber, F.G. (1967). *The principles of Teaching in the Elementary School*. Eurasia Publishing House (Pvt.) Ltd. Ramnagar, New Delhi—1.

Madry, A.E. (1963). The functions and Training needs of Adult Education Directors in Public School System. Columbus, Ohio; Ohio State University (ERIC Document Reproduction Service No. : ED 195 587).

Miller, H.L. (1964). *Teaching and Learning in Adult Education*. Macmillan Company, New York.

Murthy, S.K. (1983). *Teacher and Education in Indian Society*. Prakash Brothers; Ludhiana.

Murthy, S.K. (1982). *Philosophical and Sociological Foundations of Eduation*. Prakash Brothers, Ludhiana.

Mocker, D.W. (1974). *A Report on identification, classification, and ranking of competencies appropriate for adult basic education teachers.*

Niemi, J.A. and Davidson, C.V. (1971). The Adult Basic Education on Teacher : A Model for the analysis of Training. *Adult Leadership*. 19, p. 247.

Neiman, and James W.J. (1951). The Problems of the Concept Role — A Re-survey of the Literature. *Social Forces*, 30, No. 2 : pp. 141–149.

Otto Dahlke, H. (1958). *Values and culture and class-room*. New York : Harper and Brothers.

Oxford, R.W. (1969). *Adult Education, the Open Door, Pennsylvania*. International Text-Book Company, p. 109.

Pandey, K.P. (1958). *Constitution and Standardization of Teaching Aptitude Test*. Ph.D. Thesis, Jiwaji University.

Peck, R.F. (1959). Predicting Principals' Ratings of Teacher Performance from Personality Data. *Journal of Experimental Psychology*, 50.

Pounds, L. and Robert, L.G. (1967). *Principles of Modern Education*. New York : The McMillan Company.

Ryans, D.G. (1951). A Study of the extent of Association of certain professional and personal data with judged effectiveness of teachers behaviours. *Journal of Experimental Education*, Vol. 20, No. 1, September, 1951.

Ryans, G. (1960). *Characteristics of Teachers*. Sterling Publishers, New Delhi—6.

Robinowitz, W. and Travers, R.M.N. (1955). A drawing technique for studying certain outcomes of teachers education. *Journal of Educational Psychology*, 46, pp. 257–273.

Samantha Roy, G.K. (1971). *A Study of teacher attitude and its relationship with teaching efficiency*. Ph.D. Thesis, Sambalpur University.

Saxena, P.C. (1969). Attitudes, intelligence and personality correlates of competent teachers. *Indian Psychological Review*, 115, pp. 107–112.

Srivastava, S.S. (1974). Level of Neuroticism among different socio-economic categories. *Proceedings of the 61st Session of Indian Science Congress Section of Psychological and Educatinal Science*, Part III, 110.

Stagner, R. (1961). *Psychology of Personality*. Tokyo : Kogakusha Company Ltd.

Seaberg, (1974). *The Four Faces of Teaching : The Role of the Teacher in Humanizing Education*. Good Year Publishing Company Inc., Pacific Palisades, California.

Sherry, G.P. (1964). *A Battery of Psychological Tests for Prediction of Success in Teaching*. Ph.D. Thesis, Agra University.

Sorenson, A.G. Husek, T.R. and Yu, Constance. (1963). Divergent concepts of teacher role : An approach to the measurement of teacher effectiveness. *Journal of Educational Psychology*, LIV: pp. 287–294.

Soles, S. (1964). Teacher Role Expectations and the Internal Organization of Secondary Schools. *Journal of Educational Research*, LVII; pp. 227–238.

Stinnett, T.M. (1965). *The Professor of Teaching*. Prentice-Hall of India (Pvt.) Ltd., New Delhi.

Tripathi, V.K.D. (1972). *A Comparative Study of the Personality Profiles of Working Teachers and Teacher-Trainees.* M.Ed. Dissertation, B.H.U.

Vernon, P.E. (1957). *Personality tests and assessments.* London : Methuen & Co., Ltd.

Veri, C.C. (1968). *The design of a Doctoral Programme in Adult Education based on the Expressed Needs of Professional Practitioners.* Unpublished Doctoral Dissertation, University of Nebraska.

White, T.J. (1950). *Similarity of Training Interests among Adult Education Leaders.* Unpublished Doctoral Dissertation, University of Chicago.

Index